Emily Post
on
Second Weddings

Also in this series

Emily Post on Business Etiquette

Emily Post on Entertaining

Emily Post on Etiquette

Emily Post on Invitations and Letters

Emily Post on Weddings

EMILY POST

on

Second Weddings

Elizabeth L. Post

HarperPerennial

A Division of HarperCollinsPublishers

FIRST HARPER PERENNIAL EDITION

Designed by Kim Llewellyn

ISBN 0-06-274000-8

91   92   93   94   CC/HC   5   4   3   2   1

Contents

Introduction

In the 1920s when Emily Post published the final word on the right way to conduct oneself in any imaginable social situation, second weddings were mentioned only briefly. It was understood that if they occurred at all (and then, to be tasteful, only if the previous spouse of either or both new bride and groom were deceased), they were as private as possible, celebrated quietly, and the bride never wore white or anything resembling it. There are some who might wonder: How would Emily Post feel about an entire book in her name on this very subject?

I firmly believe that if she were here today, she would have written this book herself. The statistics in the United States alone, showing that approximately 50% of marriages end in divorce and are often immediately followed by a second (and sometimes third and fourth) wedding, demand new guidelines for addressing the complexities of how these weddings should be conducted. One of the reasons the Emily Post name has remained legend through the generations is because she understood that dramatic change in social mores required a continual new look at the rules that govern our conduct. In fact, the only rule that she, and I, have always believed to be the permanent rule of etiquette is the Golden Rule. If we all practiced daily treating others as we ourselves would want to be treated the world would be by far a kinder place to live. While that rule remains firm, rules governing weddings of all kinds have been changing throughout the century, and now more rapidly than ever.

In 1922 Emily Post introduced the concept of a morning wedding, finding it perfectly logical if the married couple should be taking an early morning train or ship directly thereafter. Naturally, a wedding at that hour produced its own set of rules, ("The bride should, of course, not wear satin and lace; she could wear organdie, or she could wear very simple white crepe de chine . . ."), just as the preponderance of second-time brides today have created the need for a fresh look at old attitudes about getting married the second time around.

This book, then, presents the 1990s' suggestions for the weddings of women and men of all ages who have rediscovered love and who want to share their commitment to making it life-long and lasting. For example, may a second-time bride wear white? Yes, she may, or she may wear white or pastels or brights or even black and white together. May she wear a traditional wedding gown? Yes, she may, just as she may wear an afternoon dress, a suit, or an evening gown. May she have a church or synagogue wedding? Yes, as long as the policy of the individual place of worship permits it.

These are some of the most-asked questions I receive from anxious second brides-to-be, along with concerns about the most graceful ways to blend families, households and finances. While many aspects of a second marriage ceremony and reception vary only slightly from a first, they are usually complicated by such things as relationships with ex in-laws, children of the bride or groom, divorced parents, and family members and long-time friends who have already celebrated (and given gifts) during the first wedding of either the bride or groom, or both.

We have come a long way since the 1920s when Emily Post wrote, ". . . Etiquette, at this moment says: 'Weddings on the Atlantic seaboard are celebrated not later than four-thirty o'clock in the afternoon.' "[!] Not only are weddings celebrated today well into the evening as well as first thing in the morning, they are celebrated with joy just because they are weddings, symbolizing hope and happiness for all those involved. Etiquette today says that whether they represent a first or a second celebration for the bride and the groom, the rules and guidelines surrounding them serve not to restrict, but to help make them elegant, tasteful and memorable for all who participate.

Elizabeth L. Post
January, 1991

Your Engagement

Q. *I am twenty-five, divorced, and plan to be married again shortly. My fiancé is thirty and has been divorced for two years. Should he talk to my parents and ask their permission and tell them our plans, or should we tell them together?*

A. Sharing this news is something you can do together, unless you know that your parents would not be in favor of the marriage. If this is the case, you should speak to them yourself, without your fiancé present, so you can explain your feelings and give them a chance to express their concerns to you. This should be followed by a talk among the four of you to "clear the air" and to share your plans. It would be reassuring to your parents to hear from your fiancé of any impact of his previous marriage has on your plans together (if he is paying alimony, whether his ex-wife might be a problem in your future relationship, etc.) You should both be open and frank with your parents, as well as with his, since they might be concerned that your past relationships would interfere with your future together.

Q. *My fiancé has two young children from a previous marriage. Who should tell them that we are going to be married?*

A. Your fiancé should tell them, without you present, so they can feel comfortable about expressing any anxieties they may have. The two of you should then talk to them together, addressing their concerns and telling them what your plans are. Children need to be reassured and informed of any changes that will affect them, and your reassurances should echo those of your fiancé.

Q. *Whom do I tell first when I become engaged to remarry, my children or my parents?*
A. You should tell your children first. Your impending marriage will have a greater impact on them than on your parents, and it is important that they hear the news from you directly, not indirectly from a grandparent or other relative. You should then immediately tell your parents, again so that they hear the news from you, not from your children!

If you are divorced and your children live with your ex-spouse, you should tell your children first so that they hear from you exactly what your plans are and how your new marriage will affect them. You do not want anyone else interpreting for you. You should then tell your ex-spouse directly. If your relationship is not amicable, you should be clear as to what the role of the children will be in your new marriage, and then you should discuss your plans, frequently, with your children so that they are not influenced by negative comments from your ex-spouse.

Q. *I am not on speaking terms with my ex-wife. I am planning to remarry. Should I tell her, or let our children tell her?*
A. You should tell her yourself, even if you haven't spoken in years. You needn't dwell on the

virtues of your fiancée or make odious comparisons between her and your ex-wife, but you should inform her of your plans. If you are planning a wedding at which you wish your children to be present or in which they will be involved, you will have to discuss this with her as well.

Q. *My ex-wife and I had a very bitter divorce and she harbors a lot of anger toward me. I am afraid that if I tell her I am going to be married again, she will try to disrupt the wedding. I want my children, who currently live with her, to be present, but don't want to involve them in a situation that forces them to lie to her. How should I handle this?*

A. Although I believe that honesty is the best policy in every situation, yours is one where that policy could cause pain or embarrassment for many people, were your ex-wife to appear at your wedding. Inform your children and your ex-wife that you are planning to remarry, without giving them the date of your wedding. Plan your wedding for a weekend or vacation time when your children would normally be visiting you, and tell your children when you pick them up. When you return your children to your wife, tell her that you were married, and that the children didn't know in advance. It is important that you prepare your children for the possibility that their mother may be angry and upset, and that you didn't tell them in advance because you didn't want them to be caught in the middle or forced to lie to their mother.

Q. *I have been a widow for many years, and now plan to be married again. My children, and my fiancé's children, are grown and have families of their own. While I have met his children, and he mine, they have never met one another. Should we bring them all together to announce our engagement?*

A. It really isn't necessary to do this at this time, nor to assume that you have to set the stage for all your children to become friends, which they may not. Since you know your fiancé's children and he knows yours, you may, as a couple, tell them separately. If you are planning to have a wedding at which they will all be present, you may want to arrange a gathering beforehand so that they can meet one another, after they have had a chance to get used to the idea that you will be married.

Q. *Both my fiancé and I are in our twenties and we are anxious for our families to meet. His mother is planning to call my parents, but since they are divorced, I don't know which one to tell her to call first. Is there some guideline for this situation?*

A. The first call is made to the parent with whom you lived after the divorce, or with whom you live now. If you are also close to your other parent, he or she should be called shortly thereafter. If your fiancé's mother wishes to extend an invitation to your parents, she should extend separate invitations and assume that they would not want to be entertained together.

Q. *My fiancé and I are both in our thirties, and both of us have been married before. We plan to have a small*

*wedding with immediate family and close friends only,
which we will pay for ourselves. In this case, should we
expect our parents (who are all in their sixties) to follow
the usual protocol and get together, with his mother
calling mine, now that we are engaged?*

A. It certainly would be gracious of your fiancé's
mother to call your mother and express her happiness at your news, which is the traditional form.
Usually, the groom's mother will suggest that the
two families meet for dinner, or arrange a weekend
visit if they live some distance from one another.
This pre-wedding meeting serves to bring the two
families together, and makes wedding planning and
arrangements (such things as guest lists and table
seating) easier for the parents of the bride and
groom. However, you and your groom might want
to arrange this yourselves, hosting a small dinner
party and including any members of your immediate families, to give them a chance to meet before
the wedding.

Q. *My widowed father is marrying a woman that my
brothers and I don't know. What is proper in this
circumstance? How do we bring up the subject of meeting her? Who makes the first call? If one of my children
were getting married, I'd know what to do, but not in
this situation.*

A. If it has not occurred to your father that you
would like to meet and welcome his future bride,
there is no reason that you can't suggest to him that
your brothers and you are looking forward to meeting her. Ask him if he has made any plans to have

you meet and if not, suggest that he bring her to one of your homes for dinner (or brunch, or lunch). It would surely please him that you approve of his plans and that you want to share them with him.

Q. *I am to be married for the second time. May our engagement be announced before I receive an engagement ring?*

A. Yes. An engagement ring is not essential to becoming engaged. If you have been given a ring, you first wear it in public on the day of the official announcement of your engagement, if one is to be made.

Q. *I'm getting a divorce and plan to remarry as soon as the divorce is final. I've already removed my wedding ring; may I wear my new engagement ring now?*

A. No, you may not. Until your divorce is final, you are still legally married to someone else and it is inappropriate to wear another's engagement ring until you are no longer legally married, even if you plan to remarry the day after your divorce is final.

Q. *I have been widowed for several years and am planning to be married again. My husband-to-be wants me to have an engagement ring. Is this proper?*

A. Of course it is proper. If you have been wearing an engagement ring from your previous marriage, you would remove it and not wear it again. You and your fiancé may want to discuss what to do with your previous engagement ring—if you have a son, you may wish to keep it to give to him to use someday as an engagement ring for his future bride—or you may wish to have the stone or stones reset and used as another form of jewelry for yourself or for your daughter. If you have continued to wear your wedding ring from your previous marriage, you may wear it until the day of your forthcoming wedding.

Q. *Is an engagement party proper for a second marriage?*
A. Certainly. Naturally you are happy with the special news you have to share with relatives and close friends, and a party celebrating your happiness is perfectly proper.

Q. *My fiancé and I are well beyond "thirtysomething." How should we announce our plans to marry to family and friends?*
A. With joy and gladness, of course, either by telephone call, personal note or letter. If you would like to announce your plans in person, you may also invite your family and friends to a cocktail party, tea, reception, brunch, or dinner, and share your news at that time. Children from previous marriages, parents, and siblings, should be told first, in person, if possible, and privately.

Q. *Who gives an engagement party and when is it held?*
A. This really depends on your ages and circumstances. A party for a young bride-to-be, even if it is her second marriage, would usually be given by

her parents or another member of her family. A party for an older couple with grown children could be given by the bride's children. It is also acceptable for the groom's family to give the party. It is usually held shortly after close family members have been informed of the engagement.

Q. *Who makes the announcement at an engagement party?*
A. The conventional announcement is made by the father of the bride-to-be, in the form of a toast. If the party is for an older couple the announcement could be made by the host of the party, whether a parent, a close friend, or a child of one of the engaged couple.

Q. *How might a toast to the future bride and groom be worded?*
A. There are many simple but lovely toasts. The person giving the toast might say, "Now you know that the reason for this party is to announce Genevieve's engagement to John. I would like to propose a toast to them both, wishing them many, many years of happiness." Another choice could be, "Please drink with me to the happiness of the couple who are so close to our hearts—Genevieve and John." A very brief toast would be, "Will you all join me in a toast to Genevieve and John?" Under no circumstances should a referral be made to a previous marriage of either member of the couple. It would be in dreadful taste to add, "and we all wish them better luck this time around" or

"if at first you don't succeed, try, try again," or "may this marriage be a more lasting one."

Q. *Are gifts given at an engagement party?*
A. Engagement presents should not be taken to an engagement party since they are not expected and may embarrass guests who have not brought anything. If given, they are generally given to the bride alone, and then only by close relatives and very special friends. Engagement gifts are not expected from casual friends and acquaintances, and they are more often given to a first-time bride than a bride who is being married for the second time. Sometimes gifts are given by the groom's family as a special welcome to the bride. Examples would be something personal, such as lingerie or jewelry, or something for the bride's linen trousseau. If gifts are taken to an engagement party, they should not be opened in front of the guests, since some may not have brought a gift.

The exception to this is in those areas or among those ethnic groups when an engagement party is held more to celebrate the engagement than to announce it. In this case, gifts are more the rule than the exception.

Q. *Are written thank you notes required for gifts given at an engagement party?*
A. Yes, assuming the gifts have not been opened in the presence of the donor. If the gifts are delivered in person and you thank the giver sincerely at the time, you need do nothing more, although a

note is always welcome. You should write notes promptly in response to all welcoming or congratulatory messages.

Q. *May I send printed engagement announcements?*
A. No, it is not in good taste to send engraved or printed announcements. You may, and should, however, send notes to or call relatives and close friends to inform them of your engagement, before an engagement party or newspaper announcement. If your engagement is to be announced at a surprise party, you may ask those to whom you write or call not to tell anyone else.

Q. *When may I announce my engagement in the newspaper?*
A. No sooner than the day after your engagement party, if you are having one. Otherwise, an announcement usually appears in the newspaper two or three months before the proposed date of the marriage, although it may appear up to a year before the wedding date, or as little as a week ahead.

Q. *Is it all right to send an announcement of our engagement to the newspaper? My fiancé has been married before, I have not.*
A. Yes, it is quite all right—the purpose of a newspaper announcement is to share your happy news with friends and acquaintances to whom you would not be making a telephone call or sending a note. In the past, a woman of forty or more did not usu-

ally announce her engagement in the newspaper for a first or second wedding, but instead called or wrote her relatives and friends shortly before the wedding. With the increase in couples marrying at a later age and with the preponderance of second weddings, this rule is no longer followed. An announcement should be sent to the society editors of the newspaper approximately two weeks before it should appear. If the announcement is to be made by your parents, the usual form is:

> Mr. and Mrs. Richard Noonan of Cross River, New York, announce the engagement of their daughter, Kendra, to Dr. Richard Armas Barnes, son of Mr. and Mrs. Michael Cuyler Barnes of New York City. Dr. Barnes' previous marriage ended in divorce. [Optional—some newspapers require this statement, most do not.] A September wedding is planned.
>
> Miss Noonan graduated from Skidmore College and is a market analyst with Hutchings and Brown in White Plains, New York. Dr. Barnes graduated from New York University and the Yale Medical School. He completed his residency at University Medical Center and is now practicing in New York City.

If the engagement announcement is to be made in your own names, it would begin:

The engagement of Miss Kendra Allison Noonan, daughter of Mr. and Mrs. Richard Noonan of Cross River, New York, to Dr. Richard Armas Barnes, son of Mr. and Mrs. Michael Culyer Barnes of New York City, has been announced.

[or]

The engagement of Miss Kendra Allison Noonan of Cross River, New York, to Dr. Richard Armas Barnes of New York City has been announced . . . etc.

In all cases, you may state that the future groom's previous marriage ended in divorce, but it is not obligatory.

Q. *Is it all right to include a photograph of the two of us with our engagement announcement?*
A. Yes, although it will be printed only if the newspaper has space and its policy permits the inclusion of photographs. The photograph used with an engagement announcement used to be of the bride alone, but today it is often a photo of the couple. A black-and-white glossy print must accompany the written information you send the newspaper.

Q. *I was married before and although divorced, retained my married name. My parents want to send an engagement announcement to the newspapers since I am going to be married again. How would my name appear, to avoid confusion?*

A. There really shouldn't be any confusion, since the relationship is clearly indicated by the wording:

> Mr. and Mrs. Charles Baldwin Vose of Westport, Connecticut, announce the engagement of their daughter, Margaret Vose Vance, to Mr. James Joseph Hulbert, son of Mr. and Mrs. Arthur Francis Hulbert of Atlanta, Georgia. Mrs. Vance's previous marriage ended in divorce. [optional] A June wedding is planned . . . etc.

Q. *There are so many names in our family that I don't know how to begin wording an engagement announcement. My parents are both divorced and remarried, and I am divorced and am planning to remarry. My parents have remained friendly and both would want to be included in the announcement. What should I do?*

A. You may word the announcement:

> Mr. and Mrs. David Hillman of Grosse Pointe, Michigan and Mr. and Mrs. Brent Fisher of West Palm Beach, Florida, announce the engagement of Mrs. Hillman's and Mr. Fisher's daughter, Amanda Fisher Tartaro, to Mr. John Lewis Clark, son of . . . etc. [optional] Mrs. Tartaro's previous marriage ended in divorce . . . etc.

Q. *My parents are divorced and are not particularly friendly. In whose name is the engagement announcement made?*

A. The mother of the bride usually announces the engagement, but the name of the other parent must be included:

> Mrs. Ruth Helmsley of Los Angeles, California, announces the engagement of her daughter, Miss Jillian Helmsley . . . Miss Helmsley is also the daughter of Mr. George Helmsley of Warrenville Heights, Ohio. . . .

Q. *My mother passed away when I was quite young. My father wants to announce my engagement in the newspaper. Would my mother be mentioned in such an announcement?*

A. Yes. When one of the bride's parents is deceased, the deceased parent is mentioned in the text of the announcement:

> Mr. [Mrs.] Edward Patrick O'Hare announces the engagement of his [her] daughter, Jennifer, to Mr. Elliot Reilly. Miss O'Hare is also the daughter of the late Mary O'Hare [Edward Patrick O'-Hare] . . . etc.

If one of the groom's parents is deceased, the form differs slightly:

> Mr. and Mrs. Harrison Brown announce the engagement of their daughter, Miss Jeanine Frances Brown, to Mr. Christopher Long, son of Mrs. Allen Carter Long and the late Mr. Long. . . .

Q. *My mother has just told us of her engagement to a long-time friend of the family. My sisters and I would like to announce their engagement. How would we word this for the newspaper?*

A. The announcement may be worded:

> The engagement of Mrs. John Quartermaine of Racine, Wisconsin to Mr. Alexander Noble of Minneapolis, Minnesota has been announced. . . .

> [or]

> The daughters of Mrs. John Quartermaine of Racine, Wisconsin, have announced Mrs. Quartermaine's engagement to. . . .

> If your mother is a divorcée and not a widow, her name would be printed "Mrs. Janice Quartermaine."

Q. *I am planning to marry a man whose divorce is not yet final. Since we will be married the minute it is, we would like to announce our engagement right away. How should we do this?*

A. You shouldn't. No announcement should ever be made of an engagement when either member is still legally married to someone else, no matter how close your planned wedding date is.

Q. *Are there circumstances under which it would be in bad taste to announce an engagement in the newspaper?*

A. Yes. It is not appropriate to send a newspaper announcement when there has recently been a death in either family or when a member of the immediate family is seriously ill. In these cases, the news is spread by word of mouth, although a public announcement may follow some weeks later.

Q. *My fiancé's family is from another town. Should an engagement announcement appear in his local paper? Should it be in his parents' name or in my parents' name?*

A. Your family should ask your fiancé's parents if they would like to have an announcement appear in their local newspapers. If so, your mother should send the same announcement that will appear in your town's papers to the papers your fiancé's parents specify.

Q. *My fiancé and I have decided that it would be a mistake to be married, but we already announced our engagement and have received some engagement presents. Should the gifts be returned? Since we already sent a notice of our engagement to the newspaper, should we send another notice saying our engagement is broken?*

A. Yes, gifts must be returned with a note:

> *Dear Nancy,*
>
> *I am sorry to have to tell you that Cole and I have broken our engagement. Therefore, I am returning the placemats that you were so sweet to send me.*
>
> *Love,*
> *Elizabeth*

A notice reading, "The engagement of Miss Elizabeth Johnson and Mr. Cole Thomas has been broken by mutual consent" may be sent to the newspaper, but it isn't obligatory.

Q. *Is it all right for my fiancé and me to open a joint checking account before we are married? Should I use my former husband's name (which I have continued to use) or simply my maiden name which I will use with my future husband's name after we are married?*

A. Yes, you may of course open a joint checking account, but you should do so with the understanding that it is for the deposit of checks you receive as engagement or wedding gifts, and you should agree that you will both draw on it only to purchase something for your future home or your joint use. The name you use should be the one for which you have legal identification and to which checks will most likely be written.

Q. *I plan to marry a woman I have known for years. I would like to reassure my children that I have made financial provision for them in my will, which will not be affected by my marriage, and that I will also be making provision to provide for her, in the event of my death. How should I do this?*

A. It is very thoughtful that you wish to make your arrangements clear to your children. Rather than making public statements to everyone at one time, find a quiet moment with each of your children and inform them of your intentions. Since, unfortunately, many children, no matter how old they may be, are hostile to their father's new wife because they feel she threatens their inheritance, your reassurance to your children should calm any anxieties they may have.

Q. *I went through a messy divorce. How do I bring up the subject of a prenuptial agreement with my future wife?*

A. Prenuptial agreements are becoming more common every day. Before speaking with your fiancée, talk to your attorney to see exactly how a prenuptial agreement is worded, what is usual to include, and how such an agreement works with your will, and how children or other family members would be affected by a disbursement of your assets. Once you are clear on the legal aspects of this agreement, you must explain to your future wife how you feel, why you feel that way, and that although you love her and plan to spend the rest of your life with her, it is important to you that you and she have an agreement as to your finances before you are wed, based on what you have gone through with your former wife.

This can be a sensitive area, and many people feel it reduces a relationship to dollars and cents, or that it predetermines that a marriage is going to fail. So you must be clear that because you were "burned" before, you feel you have to protect yourself in the event that she would, at some point, decide a divorce was necessary. You might suggest that she have a similar agreement drawn up in terms of her personal assets, because you would want her also to feel protected.

Q. *What is a trousseau?*
A. The word means a "little trousse" or bundle that the bride carries with her to the house of her husband. In the last century, a bride's trousseau included personal clothing for at least one year, as well as extensive household linens, such as sheets, pillow-cases, and table linen. Today, couples tend to buy these things together, have them already because they have lived in their own apartments or households, either independently or from a previous marriage, or receive them as wedding gifts. In fact, it is unusual for a bride today to have a "hope chest" filled with embroidered linens.

Q. *I've been married before, and at that time, I had a "trousseau." I still have all the things from my previous marriage. Should I have a trousseau for my second marriage?*
A. The three new articles a bride should have if she can possibly afford them are her wedding dress, her going-away clothes, and a nightgown and negligee for her honeymoon. Otherwise, most couples today bring with them household items they already have, augmented by wedding gifts and new purchases they make together.

Q. *My husband-to-be has been married before, but he left all the household items from that marriage with his ex-wife. I have never been married, and have been* *living at home with my parents. I really have very little, other than personal items and clothing, with which to begin our life together. My mother and aunts want to provide a trousseau for me, but I have no idea of what should be included. Have you any suggestions?*

A. This is a lovely gift, and the extent of it really depends on the life you will be leading once married. In general, you will be very well equipped if you begin your marriage with both bedroom and table linen to cover the needs of yourself and your husband, and the number of guests you may entertain during the first year of your marriage.

Q. *How should linens be marked? Do I include my former husband's last initial since I had been using that name?*

A. Since you will drop your first husband's name, you would not include his initial in any monogramming. Your initials would be those of your first name, your maiden name, and your future husband's last name, if you will be assuming his last name. Ashley Elizabeth Hopewell, who will marry George Thomas Simpson, could have linen embroidered with her married initials:

AS   [or]   *ASH*

or with her future husband's last initial:

S

When a bride chooses to keep her own name after marriage, the two last initials are used with a decorative device between:

Linen that is monogrammed before an engagement is naturally marked with the bride's maiden initials.

Q. *My husband died several years ago, and I have quite a quantity of embroidered linens, marked with his and my initials. I will remarry soon, and don't know if I should dispose of them, or keep and use them. It seems wasteful to get rid of them, since they are quite lovely and in excellent condition. What do you suggest?*
A. This is a difficult question, and the answer really depends on how your future husband would feel. Often men and women who have been married before simply merge their household items, choosing to give away or sell those things that duplicate one another and keep those things that are in the best condition, or that work well with other things they are keeping. When they make these decisions, they understand that some items may have more memories attached to them than others. If you think linens marked with your previous husband's initials would cause your future husband discomfort and that it would be better to make a fresh start together, you could certainly pack them up and save them for your children, if you have any, to use someday in their own households, or give them to your former husband's family to use.

Q. *Where are square linens marked? Rectangular ones?*

A. Square tablecloths are marked in one corner, midway between the center of the cloth and the corner, so that the monogram shows on the table.

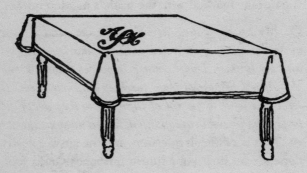

Rectangular tablecloths are marked at the center of each long side, midway between the table edge and the center of the cloth.

Very large damask napkins are marked in the center of one side, smaller ones in the corner - usually diagonally, but sometimes straight. To determine the best place to monogram napkins, fold one exactly as it will be folded for use and then make a light pencil outline in the center of the folded napkin. Give these dimensions to the store that will handle the monogramming, or use them if you are monogramming the napkins yourself.

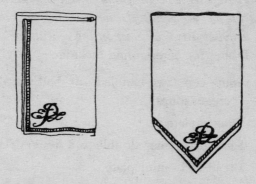

Sheets are always marked with the base of the letters toward the hem so that when the top is folded down, the letters can be read by a person standing at the foot of the bed. Pillowcases are marked approximately two inches above the hem.

Towels are marked so that the monogram is centered when the towels are folded in thirds and hung on the rack.

Q. *What are the basic requirements for everyday dishes?*
A. Usually, a complete set of 4 or 6 place settings of inexpensive china, stoneware, pottery, or un-

breakable plastic ware serves nicely as everyday dishes and meets the needs of a newly married couple.

Q. *Although my husband has been married before, I have not. He is bringing no possessions with him from his previous marriage, and we want one of our first joint purchases to be fine china for the entertaining we expect to do. We aren't sure where to begin. Could you tell us what a typical place setting consists of?*

A. Dishes for entertaining include:

> Soup cup (two-handled for both clear and cream soups)
>
> Dinner plate
>
> Salad plate (may double as a dessert plate)
>
> Bread and butter plate
>
> Cup
>
> Saucer
>
> Optional: cream soup plates, demitasse cups

Additional options are not a part of the individual place setting but do complete a set of china:

> Cream pitcher and sugar bowl
>
> Platters and vegetable dishes
>
> Gravy boat
>
> Sauce bowls for hollandaise, mayonnaise, etc.

The guidelines for selecting china is that the pieces be in harmony. They do not have to match, but they should not clash or look like a hodge-podge of bits and pieces of different sets. The harmony can be created by color or pattern. China should also match in weight—heavy earthenware does not share a table well with fine bone china.

Q. *I am a widow who is about to marry for the second time. My future husband and I have decided to splurge on sterling flatware, since neither of us have ever had it before. We are trying to decide whether to use his last name initial and both our first name initials, or my three initials. If we choose the latter, what initials do I use—my first, maiden and new last name initials, or my first, present married and future married last name initials?*

A. You may use either set, although it is customary for a widow who remarries to use her former married name as her "middle" name. For example, Susan Leigh Carr who was married to William Smith became Susan Carr Smith. When she marries Judson Moncrief, she becomes Susan Smith Moncrief. Her engraved initials, therefore, would be SSM. She may, of course, drop her former married initial and use her maiden name initial instead. In this case, Susan Leigh Carr who became Susan Carr Smith and who is marrying Judson Moncrief may become Susan Carr Moncrief. Her engraved initials, therefore, would be SCM.

Q. *How should flatware be monogrammed?*

A. Either a single letter—the initial of the groom's last name—or a triangle of letters is used for monogramming flatware. If the triangle of block letters is used, there are three variations that may be considered:

1. The last-name initial may go below with the first name initials of the bride and groom above. When Samantha Adams Burns marries Henry Wilson Carter:

2. The flatware may be engraved with the bride's married initials:

3. It may be engraved with the last-name initial above and their two first-name initials below:

If a man is a "Junior," the "Jr." is not used when the initials form a design, as on flat silver.

Any initialing should be simple in style. Elongated Roman goes well on modern silver, and Old English is best on the more ornamental styles. Monograms have usually been placed so that the top of the letter is toward the end of the handle. It appears upside down as seen by the diner at that place. Although this is traditional, it is acceptable to reverse the direction so that the initials are legible to the user, if preferred.

Q. *I have just become engaged to be married for the second time, and my fiancé and I are planning to have a moderately sized wedding. Assuming guests will give us gifts, is it inappropriate for me to use a bridal registry to assist them in their selections?*

A. No, it is not inappropriate, and is actually helpful. Often guests have no idea what to get a couple where there has been a previous marriage, thinking they surely must already have everything they need. A bridal registry is a service provided by many stores as a help to you and your friends, and you may as well take advantage of it. To use it to its best advantage, you and your fiancé should visit the stores in your area and select items you would like to have, including china, silver, and glassware patterns. The store will open a file just for you, listing the items you have chosen. When your friends shop in a store at which you have registered, the personnel can assist them by showing your choices. If a purchase is made from among the items you have indicated, that item is checked off so another friend will not duplicate the gift. As a courtesy to friends of varying means, select items in a range of prices.

Pre Wedding Events

Q. *I was married once before and am planning to be married a second time. My maid of honor wants to have a shower for me—would that be all right?*

A. If you live in the same town and have the same friends as during your first marriage, it is possible that they attended a shower for you before. In this case, it would be better to forego a shower now to which they would be obligated to bring a gift. If you are in a new area and have new friends who weren't a part of your first wedding, then a shower would not be inappropriate. This would be true, too, if you have a different job and new work friends who would like to honor you with a shower.

Q. *My future husband was married before, but I was not. My friends would like to have a shower for us, with both male and female guests. Should we say yes?*

A. Certainly. Showers that include the groom and male guests really have the feeling of a party and can be fun for the groom, who may not be involved in as many pre-wedding festivities as the bride. The guest list should not include those who were part of a shower for his first wife or friends who have given gifts in celebration of his previous marriage, unless it is made very clear that while you would love to share the celebration with them, they are not to bring a gift.

Q. *May I give my mother a bridal shower?*

A. No, it is not really proper for members of the immediate family to give showers. Instead, you could have a luncheon, tea, or cocktail party in her honor where gifts would not be expected.

Q. *Must thank you notes be written for shower presents?*
A. It is never incorrect to send thank you notes for all shower gifts received, but it is required only for those guests who have sent gifts but were not present at the time you opened them. If the bride personally thanks those in attendance as she opens their gifts, she need do no more.

Q. *I am being married for the second time and have a matron of honor and a bridesmaid as my attendants. Should there be a bridesmaid's luncheon with such a small wedding party?*
A. A bridesmaid's luncheon may be given by the bride for her attendants, or vice versa. It is simply an opportunity for you to have lunch together before the wedding, whether you have one attendant or several, and is a lovely way to share some time during what is probably a very busy period for all of you. It is usually held the weekend before the wedding so as not to conflict with work schedules, although it can be held on the afternoon of an evening wedding, especially when attendants are traveling some distance for the wedding and aren't due to arrive until that day or the day before. This get-together is a nice time for the bridesmaids to give the bride their joint gift and for her to give them their gifts.

Q. *My future stepdaughter is going to be a junior bridesmaid in my wedding. My maid of honor doesn't know if she should ask her for a contribution to their joint gift for me. Should she?*

A. Normally junior attendants are not asked to contribute to the bride's gift, but in this case she might be included since it could make her uncomfortable not to be included with the rest of the wedding party. If you think finances are a problem, alert your future husband so he can talk to her about it and advance her the funding for her contribution.

Q. *Several of our friends are planning a large dinner party for us in honor of our upcoming wedding and they are including the entire wedding party in the invitations. Should my son and my future husband's daughter, who are the ring bearer and flower girl, be invited, too?*

A. Not necessarily. Some events, such as evening showers or parties and the rehearsal dinner, may be held too late for a young child to attend. Although they are official members of the wedding party, they have no responsibilities other than those during the ceremony, and needn't be included in events which may not be appropriate either because of the type of occasion or the lateness of the hour. You and your future husband should use your own judgement as to whether or not they should be included. To prevent hurt feelings or misunderstandings, it isn't advisable to even discuss it with them if you decide they shouldn't be included.

Q. *My future husband was married before, but his friends want to give a bachelor's dinner for him. He feels funny about this. What should he do?*

A. Although a bachelor's dinner originated as a gathering of men for the purpose of bidding farewell to the groom's bachelor status, it really is similar to a bridesmaids' luncheon, serving as an opportunity for the groom, his attendants, other friends and his father and brothers to get together before the wedding. Assuming your fiancé is not currently married, he is technically a "bachelor" and shouldn't feel uncomfortable about attending a party in his honor.

Q. *My future husband has children from a previous marriage. We want to include them in as many of our wedding festivities as possible, but aren't sure what is appropriate. For example, should his daughter attend my shower? Should his sons be at his bachelor's dinner?*

A. Including your future husband's children in these events should help them to feel they are an important part of their father's new relationship with you and it would be lovely to include them, when the time of day and the occasion is appropriate for their ages. At your shower, your husband's daughter could sit with you and help you with ribbons or be responsible for tucking cards back into gift boxes. She could also go shopping with you when you select what you are going to wear, as well as what she is going to wear, for your wedding.

Your husband's sons would probably feel flattered to be invited to their father's bachelor's dinner, assuming it is not planned as a drunken revelry. If it will be less than a sedate event and his sons are young, they should not be invited. Children enjoy being able to see gifts you have received, helping you select flowers, table linens, etc. Their inclusion demonstrates to them that they matter to you and that you are beginning right away to function as a family. It is also important to have them attend the rehearsal for your wedding, so that they are prepared for the ceremony, as well as the rehearsal dinner, if possible. If children are very young, however, not really able to participate and requiring all of your and your future husband's attention, it is best not to include them in these events which are planned for you to enjoy without being torn between guests and child care responsibilities.

Q. *When is the wedding rehearsal held and who should be there?*
A. It is generally held the evening before the wedding. All members of the wedding party must be there, and the bride's parents, if they are participating. The groom's parents are not required to be there, but certainly may be if they wish.

Q. *Although my fiancé and I are having a small wedding, we will have a rehearsal beforehand and would like to give a rehearsal dinner. May we do this?*
A. Of course you may. Just because one or both of you have been married before is no reason to feel you cannot share your happiness with friends and

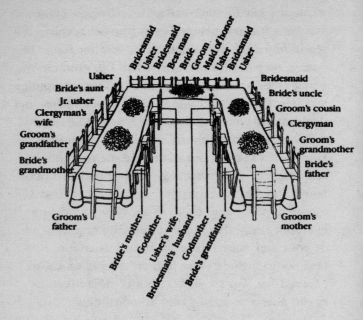

family. Usually the groom's family gives the rehearsal dinner, although a member of your family or the two of you may host it. Guests generally include the bridal party and their spouses, fiancé(e)s or live-in companions, family members and, if possible, out-of-town friends and family who arrive the day before the wedding. The clergyman, if a family friend, and his spouse, are often included.

Q. *Is there a seating order for the rehearsal dinner?*
A. When possible, all guests sit at one table. For a large dinner, a U-shaped table allows for this ar-

rangement, with guests seated both outside and inside the U. Whether the table is U-shaped, rectangular, or a large, round table, the bride sits to the groom's right with the best man to her right. The maid or matron of honor sits to the groom's left, and other attendants sit on both sides, alternating bridesmaids and ushers. Family members and friends are seated on both sides, following the wedding party. If the dinner is hosted by other than the bride and groom, the hosts sit at the feet of the U, or each at one end of a rectangular table.

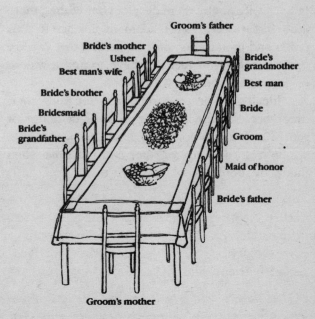

Q. *My parents were divorced and my father has remarried. I get along well with his wife. She will be attending my wedding and reception and I would like her to be at the rehearsal dinner, but because there is a small guest list, I am worried that my mother might feel uncomfortable. What should I do?*

A. Talk to your mother about your feelings and hers. If she has no problem with your father's wife attending, just be sure they are not all seated together. You might ask a brother or close relative to escort your mother so that she does not feel alone. If she is uncomfortable and would prefer that your father's wife not be there despite your wishes, there is no easy answer. If she is adamant, talk first to your father and then to his wife, explaining that you are upset but that you feel you have to find a way to respect your mother's wishes.

Ideally, divorced parents can set aside their differences for the wedding of their daughter or son. Whether it is your first or second wedding, it symbolizes a joining together and is a time when the focus should be on you, not them.

Planning Your Wedding

Q. *My future husband and I have just decided to be married. Before we even begin planning our wedding ceremony and reception, we need to plan how to integrate our children into our new family, how to work out finances, and how to combine our households. We don't even know where to begin. Is there a logical way to do all this?*

A. Yes, and you are wise to want to work these things out before beginning to plan your ceremony and reception. Your first consideration has to be your children. Today, the stepfamily is the average American family, and each comes together with ease or with difficulty, depending on the willingness of all parties to try to make it work. The children of your previous marriages have already been through either the death of a parent or a divorce, and may be unwilling to trust. They also may be worried about your loyalties to them, about having to share with new "brothers" and "sisters," and about receiving enough of your attention, whether they will live with their other parent and visit with you, or whether they will be living with you full time.

It is important that you not only tell them of your upcoming marriage before you tell anyone else, but that you include them as much as possible, according to their willingness to be included. Including them indicates that you are making a commitment not only to each other, but to them, too. Their participation should include involvement with your wedding plans and special responsibilities for them during the wedding, as well as extra time together with you as a couple.

Be prepared that blending these new relationships while adjusting to your new marriage is one of the most difficult periods for any second-time bride and groom. Allow time, in your planning, to invest in this adjustment.

Next, as to your financial and legal planning, there are several categories you should review together:

- Wills
- Insurance
- Tax Planning
- Financial Planning
- Prenuptial Agreements

Within these categories, you need to discuss whether you will open a joint bank account or have individual ones, who will contribute what to daily expenses, and how future educational costs for all of your children will be covered. It is far better to work these things out in advance than to allow misunderstanding or resentment to undermine your relationship—next to children, legal and financial areas can create the largest problems in second marriages, just as they do in first marriages.

Third, although it seems as though blending your households will be easy compared to blending your families and working out your financial relationship, it often isn't. While it should be rational and fun, it can sometimes form the basis for on-going territorial, power, and control fights. You both have to be willing to accept that some "things" have strong emotional connections, and make every effort to accommodate one another. Ideally, decisions can simply be practical ones. First, take inventory. Some things may be duplicated, others will be missing. Missing things can be bought together as a fresh start. Duplicates should, depending on space limitations, be eliminated. Be honest. If it will bother you to have a portrait of your future husband's deceased wife hanging in the dining room, say so. Don't force him to throw it out, but suggest that it could perhaps be stored and saved for one of his children. When you have made your decisions, have a garage sale or tag sale to eliminate duplicates—and agree to save the money earned for a vacation, or for new furniture you will buy to-gether.

Q. *When I was married before, I took my ex-hus-band's name but used my maiden name at work. Now that I am about to be married a second time, I don't know what to do about changing my name again. I am in the same professional field, and have two children who live with me who have their father's last name. Should I keep my old married name, assume my new married name, or change back to my maiden name?*
A. There are no specific rules, as long as you are consistent in whatever you decide. It is important to

discuss this matter with your future husband. It is likely that he (and your ex-husband) would prefer that you not retain your former married name, although you legally may (using your own first name, never your former husband's first name i.e., Mary Grant, not Mrs. John Grant). A compromise might be to use your former married name as a middle name (if you were Sarah Burns Anderson and are marrying Mark Jamison, you would become Sarah Anderson Jamison).

Since you have retained your maiden name professionally, it would make sense to continue to do so. If you want to use your new married name however, it would probably be a good idea to send a card to business associates which reads:

Judith Ann Budding
will be known as
Judith Budding Kemp
following her marriage
September 14, 1991

If you assume your future husband's last name or resume your maiden name, notify your children's school so that records can be changed and so that there is no confusion. Because this situation is so common today, most school directories list the children in alphabetical order with the parent's different last name indicated.

It is also important to notify credit card companies, banks, etc. if you change your name so that all your legal identification is identical.

It is perfectly all right to continue to use your maiden name for business and to adopt your future husband's name for social situations. In this case, no social notification is necessary. If you plan to revert to your maiden name, however, you could include an at home card with your announcements and invitations to make your preference known:

Judith Ann Budding and Frank Badart Kemp
after the first of October
20 Seagate Road, Darien, Connecticut 02650

Q. *What determines the formality of the wedding?*
A. The elements of whether a wedding is formal, semiformal or informal have traditional patterns. The chart following provides a list of your options. Many of the items are interchangeable and may be adapted to fit your situation:

Formal

Location of Ceremony	Church, synagogue, or large home or garden
Location of Reception	Club, hotel, garden or large home
Number of Guests	200 or more
Provider of services at reception	Caterer at home or club or hotel facilities
Food	Sit-down or semi-buffet (tables provided for bridal party and guests); hot meal and wedding cake

Q. *After deciding the date and site of the wedding, are there any rules about choosing the hour of the ceremony?*
A. No, there really aren't any rules, although certain customs, climates and personal preferences are "rules of thumb." For example, Catholic weddings that include a nuptial mass were traditionally held at noon or earlier to accommodate those who fasted before mass. Although this is no longer necessary, many Catholic weddings are still held at that hour. In the South, summer weddings are often held in the evening since the days are so warm. In the East, formal Protestant weddings most often are held at

Semiformal	Informal
Church, synagogue, chapel, hotel, club, home, garden	Chapel, rectory, justice of the peace, home, garden
Club, restaurant, hotel, garden, home	Church social hall, home, restaurant
75 to 200	75 or under
Caterer at home, or club or hotel facilities	Caterer, friends and relatives or restaurant
Buffet, cocktail buffet food; hot and/or cold buffet; wedding cake	Buffet; may be meal or just appetizers and wedding cake

half past four or five o'clock in the afternoon. Whatever time you choose, it is best to plan the reception to immediately follow the ceremony so that out-of-town guests are not left wondering what to do or where to go.

A wedding which takes place in the evening is assumed to be a formal wedding unless it is otherwise indicated by the wording or the style of the invitation.

Q. *When are attendants invited to be in our bridal party?*

A. As soon as you have set your wedding date, you should ask those you would like to have serve as your attendants if they would be willing to do so. You can ask them in person, by telephone or by letter.

Q. *My future husband and I are both in our 50's. This will be a second marriage for both of us, and we plan a simple, small gathering of family and close friends for our wedding. Whom should we ask to serve as our attendants?*

A. If there are children involved and they are happy about the marriage you may ask them, siblings, or close friends—whomever you would like to have share these moments with you and serve as your official witnesses to your marriage. You don't actually need attendants, but you must have witnesses who sign your marriage certificate after the ceremony.

Q. *Although my future husband has been married before, we plan to have a rather large wedding. Is there any rule about the number of ushers and bridesmaids?*

A. The only rule is really a practical rule of thumb—that there be one usher for every fifty guests. Otherwise, the average formal or semiformal second wedding party includes one or two bridesmaids and an honor attendant at the most. If it is a first wedding for the bride, four to six attendants to the bride are usual, and at least that many ushers. There may be more ushers than bridesmaids, but there should not be more bridesmaids than ushers.

Q. *May I have both a maid and a matron of honor?*
A. Yes, but the maid of honor takes precedence, holding your bouquet, being in charge of the groom's ring, and serving as a witness.

Q. *What are the responsibilities of the maid of honor?*
A. In addition to holding your bouquet and the groom's ring during the ceremony and serving as a witness, the maid of honor:

- Is the bride's "consultant," relieving the bride of as many chores as she can, especially on the wedding day
- Usually, if not a member of the bride's family, arranges for or gives a shower for the bride, often with the help of the bridesmaids
- Is in charge of choosing the gift that will be given to the bride from all the bridesmaids together, and collecting the money to pay for it
- Helps the bride arrange her gown for the recessional after the ceremony
- Stands in the receiving line
- May propose a toast to the bride and groom
- Helps the bride change into her going-away clothes
- Assists the bride's mother with any last-minute details

Q. *What are the responsibilities of the best man?*

A. At some point before the wedding, the best man consults the ushers about a gift for the groom and is then responsible for ordering it and collecting money from the ushers to pay for it. He also makes the presentation to the groom, usually at the bachelor dinner, if there is one, or at the rehearsal dinner. The best man also:

- Assists the groom in coordinating the clothing the groom, he and the ushers will wear. If it is rented formal wear, he helps the groom make sure the measurements and sizes are given to the store in plenty of time, that the ushers are fitted, if possible, and that the ushers are able to pick up their clothing
- Takes care of returning the rented clothing after the wedding
- May help the groom pack for his honeymoon
- Makes sure that the clothes the groom will change into after the wedding are packed in a separate bag and taken to the reception
- Ensures that the groom is properly dressed in plenty of time, and that he gets to the ceremony on time
- Is responsible for holding the bride's wedding ring
- Delivers the fee to the minister or rabbi on behalf of the groom

- Sees the bride and groom into their car after the ceremony, or drives them himself
- Mingles with guests during the receiving line (in which he does not stand) and helps the bride's family in any way he can
- Makes the first toast to the newlyweds at the reception
- Reads aloud, after the toast, any telegrams or messages which have been received, and delivers them to the bride's parents to keep for the couple
- Helps the groom change, toward the end of the reception, and makes sure he has everything he needs for his wedding trip
- Escorts the groom's family to the room where the groom is dressing, for their farewells
- Takes care of whatever transportation the bride and groom use to leave the reception and sees to it that their luggage is in their car
- Leads the bride and groom through the waiting guests, to the door, for their departure

Q. *Why doesn't the best man walk in the processional?*
A. In Orthodox and Conservative Jewish ceremonies the best man does precede the groom in the wedding procession, because the groom is part of the procession. In Christian ceremonies, the best man also stays with the groom but since the groom

is not part of the processional, the two enter the church through a door near the altar and the best man stays at the groom's side during the entire ceremony.

Q. *What are the responsibilities of the ushers?*
A. Very often, the groom chooses one usher who is particularly reliable or experienced to be the head usher. He is responsible for seeing that the others arrive at the rehearsal and the church on time, assigning them to certain aisles and designating the ones who will escort the immediate families of the bride and the groom. The head usher may escort the bride's and/or the groom's mothers in and out of the church or synagogue unless there are brothers of the bride or groom who are ushers, in which case they would escort their own mothers.

The ushers see that all guests and family members are seated, insofar as possible, where they wish to be. Traditionally, ushers offer their arm to women they are escorting and the women's husbands or escorts walk behind. They do not offer their arm to male guests but do walk beside them to show them to their seats. An alternative is to have the usher lead a husband and wife or other couple, walking together, to their seats and "usher" them both into it. Instead of offering his arm to the woman as a couple arrives, the usher looks at both of them and says, "Please follow me."

If there is an aisle runner or if there are pew ribbons, two ushers are appointed to be responsible for them. Ushers attend the bachelor dinner if there is one, or sometimes arrange it themselves, and they are expected to contribute to a gift for the groom. They do not stand in the receiving line, but should mingle with guests while the receiving line is in progress.

Q. *What are the age limits for flower girls, ring bearers, junior ushers and junior bridesmaids? My fiancé and I have a real age range of children between us and are unsure as to what the appropriate role is for each of them.*

A. Flower girls and ring bearers are usually between three and seven years old. Junior ushers and bridesmaids generally are between eight and fourteen, when they are too big to be flower girls and ring bearers, but too young to be bridesmaids and ushers. Depending on their size and your wishes, they may be slightly older or younger.

Q. *What are the responsibilities of younger attendants and what do they wear?*

A. Flower girls used to scatter petals before the bride, but more often today they simply carry a basket or bouquet of flowers. A flower girl must be part of the rehearsal, but whether she is included in showers and the rehearsal dinner depends on her age and the wishes of her parents. Her dress is paid for by her family. It may be similar to the bridesmaids' dresses or it may be modified to a child's style, in a complementary or matching color.

A ring bearer carries the ring or rings, fastened

to a firm white velvet or satin cushion with a white thread or a hat pin. Often, facsimiles are on the cushion and the best man and maid of honor carry the real rings. Like the flower girl, the ring bearer must attend the rehearsal, but his attendance at other functions is optional. The most appropriate dress for a ring bearer is short pants and an Eton jacket, preferably white, but occasionally navy. A miniature version of the ushers' apparel is not appropriate.

Junior ushers, if there are two of them, are often appointed to be in charge of the aisle runner or the pew ribbons. Otherwise, their only duties are to attend the rehearsal and to be part of the processional and recessional. They walk behind the regular ushers and dress like them.

Junior bridesmaids, like junior ushers, are responsible only to walk in the procession. They attend the rehearsal, but they are not expected to give showers or to contribute to the bride's gift (except in the case when a junior bridesmaid is your or your fiancé's daughter, in which case she would feel more included if she participated in the gift). Junior bridesmaids need not stand in the receiving line, but may do so if asked to by the bride. Their attendance at the rehearsal dinner and at showers is not mandatory, although again, if they are the daughters of the bride or groom, making sure they are invited is a special way to include them in the events surrounding your wedding. Junior bridesmaids dress like the bridesmaids.

Q. *My future husband and I each have children who will live with us after we're married. We are anxious to include them in the wedding ceremony. How may we do so?*

A. Older children may serve as maid of honor or best man, as ushers or bridesmaids, or as junior ushers or junior bridesmaids. Very young children could be included as ring-bearer or flower girl, although it is important to include all children and not just some. Ask your minister or rabbi to alter the vows to allow all your children to say "we will," or "we do," in response to his question "Who will support this new family?" or "Who gives this woman?" It is also lovely if, just before the recessional, you each or an older brother or sister hold the hands of little ones as you walk back down the aisle as a new family.

If you are not having attendants, children may read a special verse or a lesson, or light a candle during the ceremony.

It is also important to have special tasks for them so they feel included throughout the reception—greeting guests, or attending to the guest book, for example. They may also be a part of the receiving line, even if they aren't in the wedding party, if this would make them feel an important part of your ceremony.

Do consider the feelings of your former spouses when making these plans, however. If your relationships are amicable, it is wise to discuss your wishes with them before talking to the children so that you have their support. If your relationships are hostile, you have to handle this in a way that does not create problems for your children, either beforehand or afterward, which usually means explaining that both of you want them to be in your wedding, but that their other parent does not so that they have a choice. If they choose not to participate directly, then it is important that you don't upset them with your disappointment and that you include them in sharing times before and after your wedding.

Q. *May either my oldest son or my two daughters walk me up the aisle?*

A. Yes, they may. It used to be that only the father of the bride, or in his absence an older male relative or close friend, served as escort to the bride. Today it is perfectly acceptable for the bride to walk alone, to have her children escort her, (whether sons *or* daughters), or in the case of a younger bride, her mother or a favorite aunt or friend. It is preferable to have only one or at most two of your children escort you, simply because the aisles are narrow and you don't want to look like a crowd when you are making your entrance.

Q. *My parents were divorced when I was little and both have remarried. I've grown up with my mother and stepfather, but still keep in close contact with my natural father. Who should walk me up the aisle? I don't want to hurt either one's feelings.*

A. It is the natural father's prerogative, if he has remained close to his daughter to walk her up the aisle. There are many exceptions but that is the rule and it can give the bride a guideline to fall back on and serves to avoid hurting her stepfather's feelings. In rare instances, both may escort you together but be sure you share your plans with each so one doesn't assume he will be escorting you alone. If your communication is open with both, there is nothing wrong with presenting your concerns to them and telling them you don't know what to do. It is likely that one will defer to the other and come up with the best solution. Another possibility, if one is helping to pay for your wedding and the other is not, to have the father who is assisting financially escort you, which would be understood by the other. You could also consider having the one who does not escort you participate in the ceremony by reading a verse or selection that is meaningful to you.

Q. *Is it appropriate to have my children answer when the minister asks, "Who giveth this woman?"*

A. Yes, although in today's day and age, this question is being asked less and less during marriage ceremonies. This question may be left out of your ceremony (be sure to tell your minister you do not wish it included). Or it may be rephrased, as mentioned before, to, "Who will support this new family," in the case of a blended family with young children, or "Who will support this marriage?" if you would like your children of any age to participate and to respond.

Q. *I was married once before, and my then-husband and I eloped. This time, I want a real wedding with a gown and a church and a reception. My mother says I can't wear a white gown because I've been married already. Is she right?*

A. It once was that a white gown was considered a symbol of the virginity of the bride. This is no longer true, and a white gown is considered the symbol for a joyful wedding celebration. Colored accessories and/or flowers can be lovely and appropriate and indicate that you are not a first-time bride. This does not mean you have to wear a white gown—depending on the formality of your wedding, a suit, beautiful day dress, or off-white or pastel gown are equally good choices. Blusher veils, even in the 1990s, still do symbolize virginity, so they are not used in a second wedding unless demanded by religious custom. Alternatives are flowers, hats, or draped veiling. A second-time bride usually forgoes a train as part of her gown.

Q. *My fiancé is in the military. Should he wear his uniform for our wedding?*

A. If it is important to him and you approve, he certainly may wear his uniform, but he is not required to do so.

Q. *I didn't get married in a church for my first marriage, but I want to for my second. Would it be proper for me to wear a bustier type dress with no sleeves or neckline in a church?*

A. The answer to your question has to be given by your minister or rabbi. Some churches and synagogues have guidelines for attire which take precedence over personal preference. If there is no such objection, there is no reason you cannot wear the type of gown you describe.

Q. *My mother is planning to be married soon. Should she wear a wedding dress? What sort of outfit should she wear if not?*

A. A woman of 40+ usually does not look her best in a traditional wedding gown. Depending on the time of day for your mother's wedding, she should instead consider a formal evening gown, a tea-length or short afternoon dress, a dressy suit, or a dinner or cocktail dress. Although any of these choices may be white, usually an off-white or soft pastel shade is most flattering.

Q. *We are planning a "black and white" wedding, but I don't know what my future husband's young daughter who will be our flower girl should wear. Black seems severe, but an all-white dress may make her look like a little bride. Do you have any suggestions?*

A. A small black and white check, pin stripe, plaid or floral print would fit in with your theme without being either too harsh or too "bridey." Whatever you select should be age-appropriate and not too grown-up for a young child.

Q. *I am planning to wear a traditional wedding gown, even though this is my second wedding. Are there any guidelines as to what my attendants, my mother and the groom's mother should wear?*

A. Yes, there are. As for a first wedding, there is

correct attire for every type of wedding, whether daytime or evening, informal or formal. Following is a chart which will enable you to see at a glance what is appropriate for members of the wedding party, parents of the bride and groom, and for guests, as well as for a second-time bride. A wedding which is a first wedding for the bride would include a veil and train as options, neither of which are generally worn by a second-time bride:

	Most Formal Daytime
Bride	Long white, off-white or pastel dress; gloves optional; flowers, floral headpiece or hat
Bride's attendants	Long dresses, matching shoes; gloves are bride's option
Groom, his attendants, bride's father or step-father	Cutaway coat, striped trousers, pearl gray waistcoat, white stiff shirt, turndown collar with gray-and-black-striped four-in-hand or wing collar with ascot, gray gloves, black silk socks, black kid shoes

Q. *What type of bouquet may I carry?*

A. Your bouquet should complement what you are wearing in size and style. For example, if you are wearing a short dress, you would not want a cascading bouquet that would extend below the hem of your dress. For flowers, avoid orange blossoms, which are heavily symbolic for first time brides. Otherwise you may carry white or pastel flowers or a combination of both as your bouquet. A basket of

Most Formal Evening	Semiformal Daytime
Same as most formal daytime	Long white, off-white or pastel dress; headpiece or hat and gloves optional
Same as most formal daytime	Same as most formal daytime
Black tailcoat and trousers, white piqué waistcoat, starched-bosom shirt, wing collar, white bow tie, white gloves, black silk socks, black patent-leather shoes or pumps or black kid smooth-toe shoes	Black or charcoal sack coat, dove gray waistcoat, white pleated shirt, starched turn-down collar or soft white shirt with four-in-hand tie, gray gloves, black smooth-toe shoes

	Most Formal Daytime
Mothers or stepmothers of couple	Long or short dresses; hat, veil or hair ornament; gloves optional
Women guests	Street-length cocktail or afternoon dresses (colors are preferable to black or white); gloves and head covering, optional
Men guests	Dark suits; conservative shirts and ties

Most Formal Evening	Semiformal Daytime
Usually long evening or dinner dress, dressy short cocktail permissible; veil or hair ornament if long dress; small hat, if short; gloves optional	Long or street-length dresses, gloves and head covering, optional
Depending on local custom, long or short dresses; if long, veil or ornament— otherwise, hat optional; gloves optional	Short afternoon or cocktail dress; head covering for church optional
If women wear long dresses, tuxedos; if short dresses, dark suits	Dark suits

	Semiformal Evening
Bride	Same as semiformal daytime
Bride's attendants	Same length and degree of formality as bride's dress
Groom, his attendants, bride's father or stepfather	Winter, black tuxedo; summer, white jacket; pleated or piqué soft shirt, black cummerbund, black bow tie, no gloves, black patent-leather or kid shoes
Mothers or stepmothers of couple	Same as semiformal daytime
Women guests	Cocktail dresses, gloves and head covering for church, optional
Men guests	Dark suits

Informal Daytime	Informal Evening
Short afternoon dress, cocktail dress, or suit	Long dinner dress or short cocktail dress or suit
Same style as bride	Same style as bride
Winter, dark suit; summer, dark trousers with white linen jacket or white trousers with navy or charcoal jacket; soft shirt, conservative four-in-hand tie; hot climate, white suit	Tuxedo if bride wears dinner dress; dark suit in winter, lighter suit in summer
Short afternoon or cocktail dresses	Same length dress as bride
Afternoon dresses, gloves and head covering for church, optional	Afternoon or cocktail dresses, gloves and head covering for church, optional
Dark suits; light trousers and dark blazers in summer	Dark suits

Semiformal
Evening

Groom's father or stepfather: He may wear the same
  costume as the groom and his attendants,
  especially if he is to stand in the receiving line. If
  he is not to take part and does not wish to dress
  formally, he may wear the same clothes as the
  men guests.

---

flowers or a nosegay are more appropriate for
younger brides than older ones. A single flower or
a flower and a prayer book, however, are lovely
choices for brides of any age, and a corsage is appropriate for a simple ceremony when the bride is
wearing a suit or a dress.

Q. *Are boutonnieres the same for all men in the bridal
party?*
A. No. The ushers wear one kind of flower, usually carnations. The best man and the fathers may
wear carnations, too, or a gardenia. The groom
generally wears a different flower from those of the
other men, such as a sprig or two of lily of the
valley, a gardenia if the others are not wearing
them, or stephanotis.

Q. *What decorations may be used for a church wedding?*
A. The decision really depends on several factors,
such as the size and style of the church, the formal-

Informal Daytime	Informal Evening

Groom's father or stepfather: He may wear the same costume as the groom and his attendants, especially if he is to stand in the receiving line. If he is not to take part and does not wish to dress formally, he may wear the same clothes as the men guests.

---

ity of the wedding, the cost, and the regulations of the church itself.

A large sanctuary with high ceilings needs many tall floral arrangements to have them show up at all. Even in a small church or chapel, remember that the flowers are seen from some distance and bolder flower varieties in simple, clear arrangements show up better than small blossoms.

The color of the flowers should, if possible, coordinate with the bride's flowers or with the dresses and flowers of the bridal attendants.

Some choices include two arrangements of flowers on the altar and/or in a spray on either side of the chancel steps, for a church. In addition, a cluster of flowers, a cascade of greens, ribbons, or a fall of flowers and ribbons may be used to decorate the ends of all or some of the pews.

Q. *Because both of us have been married before, we prefer to have a very small wedding. However, the ceremony will be held in a large church. Is there any way we can make it seem more intimate?*

A. One effective decorating technique is to rent pots of shrubbery to form a "hedge" in front of the pews that will not be occupied. If the altar, chancel and occupied pews are brightly lighted and the area behind the screen of greens is left almost dark, the part of the church you are using will seem more intimate. Although your guests would use the aisle, the wedding party would enter from the side rather than proceeding down the long, dark aisle. Or, if there are choir stalls in the front, use them as pews and have only the chancel lighted. This gives the smallest weddings all the solemn beauty of church surroundings in a warm environment.

Q. *What should be done with flowers from the ceremony after the wedding?*

A. There are several thoughtful ways to share the flowers from your wedding. You may donate them to the church or synagogue if your wedding is the day before usual services. If you would like to do this, be sure to let the minister or rabbi know so that other flowers are not ordered for that day. You could also have them delivered to a hospital or nursing home to be given to people who need cheering up, or send some of the flowers to a close friend or relative who is not able to attend because of illness.

Q. *This is my second wedding, and my future husband and I have decided to have a large guest list and several attendants. Because my first wedding was so small, I only had my sister as an attendant and she wore a dress she already owned. Before I ask friends to be my attendants for this wedding, I need to know what I am really asking. Who pays for their gowns, their hotel rooms, etc? And who pays for my future husband's attendants?*

A. Your attendants are expected to pay for the clothing and accessories they wear to be in your wedding, even though what they wear is your decision. They also are expected to pay their own travel costs, but you are expected to pay for hotel accommodations or to make arrangements for lodging for them with friends, neighbors or relatives. You also pay for their bouquets or flowers, and make the arrangements for their transportation from where they are staying to the church or synagogue, to the reception, and back to the place they are staying. It is customary for bridal attendants to contribute toward a gift for the bride, and for the bride to give a gift to each of her attendants.

Groomsmen pay the charge for the rental of their own wedding attire, and the cost of transportation to and from the city or town where the wedding takes place. They contribute to a gift from all of them to the groom, and participate in the expenses of a bachelor dinner, if they are the hosts. The groom pays the cost of the lodging for his attendants, for their boutonnieres and for their ties and gloves, if they need to be purchased rather than rented. The groom also pays for transportation to the church or synagogue, and for a gift for each of his attendants.

Q. *Who pays for the lodging expenses for family or friends when they come from out of town?*

A. They pay their own expenses, although either the bride or groom or their immediate family may arrange lodging with other friends or relatives, or secure hotel accommodations, as a courtesy. You may offer to pay the expenses of out-of-town guests, but it is neither expected nor required.

Q. *My fiancé has been married before, but his parents want to contribute financially to our wedding. Is there a guideline for what should be my parents' expenses and what should be theirs?*

A. Traditionally, the bride and her family pay for:

- Invitations and announcements
- Bride's wedding dress and accessories
- Floral decorations for the church and the reception
- Bouquets for the bridesmaids
- Bouquet for the bride (unless local custom is that it is provided by the groom)
- Corsages for the bride's mother and grandmothers, unless the groom is providing them
- Boutonniere for the bride's father
- Music during the ceremony and the reception
- The facility or sexton's fee
- Transportation for the bridal party to the ceremony and then to the reception if rented limousines are used

- All the expenses of the reception
- Bride's presents to her attendants
- Bride's present to her groom, if she wishes to give him one
- Groom's wedding ring
- Hotel accommodations for bride's attendants if they cannot stay with friends, neighbors or relatives
- Travel expenses and lodging for the priest or rabbi if he or she has been invited by the bride's family and must travel some distance to perform the ceremony
- Formal wedding photographs and candid pictures, and the cost of a videographer, if used
- Ribbons and an aisle runner for the ceremony, if desired, and if not provided by the church or synagogue
- The services of a traffic officer, if necessary

Traditionally, the groom and his family pay for:

- Bride's engagement and wedding rings
- Groom's present to his bride, if he wishes to give her one
- Gifts for the best man and the ushers
- Hotel accommodations for the groom's attendants if they can't stay with friends, neighbors or relatives
- Ties, gloves and boutonnieres for the groomsmen
- Groom's and his father's boutonnieres

- Minister's or Rabbi's fee or donation
- The marriage license
- Transportation for groom and best man to ceremony
- Expenses of the honeymoon
- All costs for the rehearsal dinner
- Bride's bouquet in areas where it is the custom
- Bride's going-away corsage
- Corsages for immediate members of both families, unless the bride has included them in her florist order
- Bachelor dinner, if he wishes to have one
- Lodging and transportation for groom's parents
- Travel expenses and hotel accommodations for the minister or rabbi if he or she has been invited by the groom's family and must travel some distance to perform the ceremony

It is important to remember that these are long-standing, traditional guidelines. A bride and groom planning a second wedding most often pay the expenses themselves, since it is probable their parents contributed to their first wedding. Parents have no obligation to pay for their children's wedding expenses, but sometimes will offer to cover a particular expense, or to cross the traditional boundaries and contribute to expenses usually covered by the other family. The children of older couples marrying for the second time sometimes pay the expenses of the wedding as a gift to their parents. What is important is that you know, as you plan, what your anticipated costs are and who is paying for what portion of it so that you do not overextend yourselves financially.

Q. *How much should the pastor or rabbi's fee be?*
A. The amount varies according to the size and the formality of the ceremony. It may range from $50 for a small, private wedding to from $100 to $300 for an elaborate one. If the fee is paid by check, it is made out to the pastor or rabbi unless he or she has informed you it should be made out to the church or synagogue instead. If your pastor has traveled any distance to perform the ceremony at the invitation of either family both traveling and lodging expenses are paid for by the family at whose request the trip was made.

Q. *Who decides on the number of guests to be invited?*
A. This is determined by whoever is hosting the wedding reception since it becomes a financial decision, as well as a decision based on the size and type of reception you want.

Q. *I have not been married before. My fiancé has. My parents are excited about our wedding and have offered to pay for it. How do we divide the total number of invitations between my family and his?*
A. Naturally, a certain number of invitations are first set aside for friends of the couple. Then the

reminder are usually divided in half, especially if both families are of roughly equal size and if they live in the same community. If they do not, your fiancé's mother will have an idea of how many of the groom's family and friends will travel to attend a second wedding for her son, and she should give this information to your mother. If the number of invitations she requires are fewer than half, your mother may use the remainder.

Q. *What should we anticipate discussing with our pastor when we first meet with him?*
A. There are several points to cover, depending on your religion. A general checklist includes the following:

- The service itself—whether it will be traditional and/or whether you wish to write your own vows or special passages
- Whether you or he should contact the organist about music
- Your preferred date and time for your wedding and a time for the rehearsal
- What, if any, papers or documents he may need from you
- Whether photographs may be taken during the ceremony
- Whether candles may be used
- A recommendation on the number of guests the church or synagogue will hold
- With whom you should discuss such things as canopies, carpets, dressing facilities, etc.
- The various fees for use of the church or

synagogue, the sexton, the organist, and for the minister
- Whether there are any dress restrictions for the wedding party
- Whether decorations are permitted, and if so, when you or your florist can have access to decorate

Additionally, your pastor will want to set up counseling sessions for you both to meet with him or her. As a second-time bride or groom, you may be faced with complex family relationships, and certainly with residual emotions from previous marriages. Your pastor will want to talk to you about how you both face problems, how you communicate, what your expectations are for your marriage, and what you expect the dynamics of your relationship to be.

Q. *May a relative who is a member of the clergy perform my wedding?*
A. Yes, as long as you ask your minister's approval for this arrangement. If he or she agrees, you and your fiancé should talk with both of them, or communicate by telephone or letter, to make all arrangements. You may want to ask your minister to assist your relative during the ceremony, and to determine which of them will conduct counseling sessions with you.

Q. *Although we are having a small wedding, we would like to hire a photographer to capture all the* *special moments on film. When should we select him or her, and what should we discuss?*

A. You should reserve a photographer's time as soon as possible after you have confirmed the date, time and place of your ceremony and reception. You may ask to see his or her portfolio and discuss the kinds of pictures you wish to have—both candid and formal. Your formal portrait, should you wish to have one, is taken as soon as your wedding dress is ready—at least three weeks before the ceremony. This is especially important if you wish to have a picture of yourself in your bridal gown appear in the newspaper.

You should really like the style of candid photographs he or she shows you. If his or her tendency is to superimpose your photograph onto another so it looks as though you are standing in a champagne glass or on top of your wedding cake and your wishes are for truly candid shots of you and your guests, you won't have a good match unless you are sure he understands what *you* want.

Discuss the schedule of the day with the photographer, including when you would like pictures taken, whether you want formal pictures of the bridal party, and when they should be taken. Also make your feelings known about photographs during the ceremony: that no flash be used or noise made if pictures are taken; and be sure that the photographer does not stand where he or she would block the view of your guests.

Naturally you should discuss cost and obtain a written estimate or contract. It is possible to negotiate changes in the photographer's usual package. For example, if you and your groom are in your 60's, it is unlikely that you want the usual albums for parents. Instead, you may be able to trade those for all the proofs, or for additional sizes, etc. Include the following questions in your discussion:

- What does a wedding "package" consist of?
- What is the cost for additions?
- How many photographs are included in the cost?
- What is the number of pages in the photographer's standard wedding album?
- What does it cost per extra album page?
- What is the size and cost of extra albums?
- What is the cost of keeping proofs?

Some photographers expect beverages and a meal at the reception. Be sure to check this cost with your caterer before discussing it with the photographer.

If you are considering having your ceremony and reception videotaped, be sure to first ask the minister or rabbi if videotaping is permitted during the ceremony. Then ask to preview a sample of the videographer's work at other weddings before discussing terms with him or her. Ask the same kinds of questions you would ask a still photographer and explain specifically what you want covered.

Q. *What type of music may we have at the ceremony? May we include some of the more traditional wedding music?*

A. Many churches and synagogues do not permit secular music during ceremonies which means that even if "Theme From A Summer Place" is your favorite song and the first one you danced to together, it may not be played during the ceremony and should be saved for the reception. Usually, traditional classical music is permitted, and any of the more traditional, classical wedding music is appropriate. If you have no particular preference and are unsure what to select, consult with the organist who will be able to make several recommendations and who will know what the rules of the church or synagogue will permit.

Q. *When and how should we select musicians for the reception?*
A. As soon as you set your wedding date you should hire the musicians. The size and formality of your reception determines the type of music you plan. It may be provided by anything from a tape deck to a single pianist to a ten-piece band.

　　If you don't know where to begin, the caterer can often make recommendations. Also check the Yellow Pages, ask friends, or call the local musicians union. To be sure you will be getting the music and musicians you think you are hiring, ask for a schedule of other appearances the musicians or disk jockey you are considering will be making so you can listen to them before making your choice.

　　When discussing terms, include the length of the reception, their price, the cost of overtime should you wish to extend the reception, specific songs you would like played and the number and length of the breaks they will take. Often band members or musicians expect beverages and/or a meal, which is something you should discuss with your caterer.

Q. *Is there any kind of check list I should be following in advance of my wedding?*
A. At least three months in advance of your wedding:

- Set the date and hour for the ceremony with your minister or rabbi, and for the reception
- Engage the caterer, club, or restaurant you have selected
- Select attendants and ask them to serve
- Make out your tentative guest list
- Finalize the list, and order your invitations and announcements
- Order what you will wear, and what your attendants will wear
- Talk to your minister or rabbi and organist about music, decorations, and procedure (such as whether photographs are allowed, and the time of the rehearsal)
- Engage the services of a florist
- Make appointments with photographers and musicians
- Set a date to have a formal portrait taken
- Hire the musician(s)
- Hire limousines, if required, for transport-

ing the bridal party to the ceremony and
then to the reception
- If your wedding is to be at home, make arrangements for repairs and cleaning
- If you wish, order notepaper for thank-you
notes monogrammed with your present initials, and with your married initials for later

Two months before your wedding:

- Notify attendants about fittings, and accessories. If possible, have shoes dyed in one lot
- Select gifts for your attendants and for your
groom, if you intend to give him one
- Register at local department or gift store
bridal registries
- Meet with the caterer, club, or restaurant
manager to discuss menu, seating arrangements, linen colors, parking, etc.
- Mail invitations four to six weeks before
your wedding

One month before your wedding:

- Check with your groom about his blood test
and the marriage license
- Record all gifts and write thank-you's as
they arrive
- Check on all accessories for you and your
attendants
- Make final arrangements with the profes-
sionals who are working with you—florist,
photographer, musicians, caterer

- Arrange to change your name (if you are doing so) and address on all documents, such as your driver's license, credit cards and checking account
- Arrange for a bridesmaids' luncheon if you wish to give one
- Address announcements and prepare them for mailing the day after your wedding
- Make arrangements for a place for the bridesmaids to dress. It is best if they are all together, whether in your home, at a friend's house, or in a room in the church or synagogue
- Plan reception seating and make out place cards if you will be using them
- Send your wedding announcement and portrait to the newspapers

Invitations
& Announcements

Q. *When should invitations be ordered?*
A. As soon as you have confirmed dates and times for both the ceremony and the reception. Engraved or thermographed invitations usually take at least three months to print.

Q. *How far in advance of the wedding are invitations sent?*
A. Approximately ten days to three weeks for an informal wedding and four to six weeks for a formal one.

Q. *We are going to have a small wedding followed by a barbecue, but would like to send formal invitations. Is this all right?*
A. The style of your invitations should match the formality of the wedding. All elements should be consistent for a smooth and harmonious sense, and your invitations set the tone of the ceremony. Therefore, it would be preferable that your invitations be as informal and personal as your ceremony and reception will be.

Q. *We are planning a very small gathering of friends and family for our wedding, which is the second for my husband. May we telephone invitations to those we would like to invite?*
A. Yes, you may. Telephoned invitations are also a solution if you decide to marry with little advance notice.

Q. *Are informal notes ever used as wedding invitations?*

A. Yes, when the wedding is small and informal, notes may be written by hand. Suggested wording would be:

> *Dear Jason and Cecily,*
>
> *Martin and I are to be married at Norfolk Presbyterian Church on April 12th at four thirty. We hope you both will come to the church, and afterward to the reception at Hilltop Country Club.*
>
> *With much love from both of us,*
>
> *Liz*

Q. *My fiancé and I would like to send an invitation that is neither formal nor just a handwritten note. Is it proper to design and write our own, with our own wording?*

A. Yes, you may do this. It is as informal as a handwritten note, and should be used particularly when you are inviting less than 50 guests or are planning a small, intimate wedding. One example of a card written in the bride's hand follows:

Lee Spencer and Peter Davis

invite you to
celebrate their
marriage

on
Saturday, September
the eighth
at four o'clock

44 Beach Road, Essex, Connecticut

R.S.V.P.

Q. *I use a different name professionally than I do socially, and am worried that if I use other than my professional name invited guests with whom I work won't know who I am. Should I order two sets of invitations?*

A. No, you may instead print your given name first, and then identify your professional name:

Linda Stephens Horn

(Linda Thomas)

Q. *We would like to have printed invitations, but don't want to use the traditional wording. May we select a variation, or are we stuck with the standard?*

A. You may use a variation on the traditional, centered, formal style, so long as the wording is in good taste. You should look through sample books of invitations at a printer for ideas, or you may consider one of the following:

Katherine Newberry

and

Reid Cole

invite you to share in the joy

of the beginning of a new life together

when they exchange vows of marriage

Saturday, the fourteenth of February

at seven o'clock in the evening

Christ Episcopal Church

Miami, Florida

[or]

Our joy will be more complete
if you can share in the ceremony
of our marriage
Friday, the sixth of March
at eleven o'clock in the morning
at St. John's Lutheran Church
and celebrate with us
during the reception following
The Pines
Mamaroneck, New York

Susan Foltin and Richard Hahn

The same type of invitation may be issued by the bride's or the groom's parents instead of by the bride and groom:

Our joy will be more complete
if you will share in the marriage of our daughter
Susan Foltin
to
Mr. Richard Hahn
at half after four o'clock
6 West Avenue
Greens Lane, Pennsylvania
We invite you to worship with us
witness their vows and join us
for a reception following the ceremony
If you are unable to attend, we ask your
presence in thought and prayer
Mr. and Mrs. William Briar
[or, Anne and William Briar]

R.S.V.P.

Q. *To include our children in our wedding, my future husband and I want to issue the invitations in conjunction with our children. How can we include them in the invitation?*

A. One suggestion for this lovely thought follows:

Thomas Lane and Joyce Payton
together with their children
request the honour of your presence at
their wedding
on
Saturday, July 17
at three o'clock
Westlakes Community Church

Q. *We know the hosts of the wedding reception issue the invitations. My future husband and I are having a small wedding at our church. Because we are anxious that our new blended family gets off on the right foot we'd like to issue invitations in our children's names. Would it be proper for our invitations to read:*

> *Alexander, Adam, Joshua and Brittany Morgan*
> *and*
> *Peter and Cynthia Anderson*
> *request the honour of your presence*
> *at the marriage of their parents*
> *Jean Collins Morgan*
> *and*
> *Geoffrey Daniel Anderson*
> *[etc.]*

A. Yes, it would be proper and is a lovely way to show your unity as a new family, and perhaps to introduce your children to one another's friends and family.

Q. *Is it proper to send a wedding invitation by FAX?*
A. I suppose in the future the FAX will become the solution for brides who wish to communicate instantly, but they still are found primarily in business offices and not in homes. Information sent by FAX to someone's office should not be of a personal nature, which rules out using them for social invitations at present. The exception would be if you decided to marry immediately and could not reach

an invited guest by telephone or by mail in time to give them notice. Otherwise, I would strongly recommend a telephone call or handwritten note rather than an invitation by FAX.

Q. *We don't want guests to send gifts to us. We have both been married before, have everything we need, and just want our family and friends to celebrate with us, not to feel obligated to send or bring a gift. May we put, "no gifts, please" on our invitations?*

A. You may, but since it is understood that second marriages do not demand a gift, it isn't necessary to add this line. Close friends and relatives who want to give you a gift will do so whether you add this line or not; other recipients would not, or should not, assume you are expecting gifts just because you don't include this disclaimer on the invitations. You may also add the words "in lieu of gifts contributions may be made to [the charity of your choice] in honor of the bride and groom."

Q. *What is the wording for a formal second wedding invitation?*

A. There is no difference between the wording guidelines for an invitation to a first wedding and an invitation to a second wedding. Both have standard formats for the traditional, engraved or thermographed style:

- The invitation to the wedding ceremony reads, "requests the honour (spelled with a u) of your presence . . ."

- The invitation to the reception, when not an enclosed card reading "reception following the ceremony," reads, "requests the pleasure of your company . . ."
- No punctuation is used except after accepted abbreviations, such as "Mr.," "Mrs.," etc., or when phrases requiring separation occur in the same line, as in the date
- Numbers and dates are spelled out, but long numbers in the street address may be written in numerals
- Half hours are written as "half after four," never "half past four" nor "4:30 P.M." Use "in the evening" or "in the morning instead of "a.m." or "p.m."
- The full name of the recipient is written out. The use of an initial—"Mr. and Mrs. Mark H. Coleman"—is not correct. Either the middle name should be written, if known, or eliminated
- "Doctor" is written in full, but "Mr." is never written "Mister." "Junior may be written in full, although "Jr.," is preferred
- No words are capitalized except those that would be ordinarily, such as people's names and titles, place names and names of the day and month
- The year does not have to be included on wedding invitations, but usually is on announcements since they may be sent long after the wedding takes place

- The invitation to the wedding ceremony alone does not include an R.S.V.P.
- On the reception invitation, "R.S.V.P.," "R.s.v.p." and "The favour of a reply" are equally correct. If the address to which the reply is sent differs from that which appears on the invitation, it is also correct to use "kindly send reply to," followed by the correct address

Q. *What is the traditional style of an invitation?*
A. Traditional invitations are engraved or thermographed on the first page of a double sheet of ivory, white or soft cream heavy paper. The paper may be flat or have a raised margin. Separate invitations to the reception are engraved on small, stiff cards appropriate in size to the size of the wedding ceremony invitation.

Q. *What is the correct form for an invitation to the wedding ceremony only?*
A. The most formal wedding invitation, rarely seen today, has the name(s) of the recipient(s) written by hand:

Doctor and Mrs. John Huntington Smith
request the honour of

Mr. and Mrs. Edward Fitzgerald's

presence at the marriage of
their daughter Millicent Jane
to
Mr. James Edward Pope
Saturday, the first of November
at twelve o'clock
St. John's Church

R.S.V.P.

An equally correct and more commonly used form is:

Doctor and Mrs. John Huntington Smith
request the honour of your presence
at the marriage of their daughter
Elaine Smith Scott
[etc.]

Q. *Our guest list for the ceremony is larger than for the reception. Do we need a separate invitation to the reception?*

A. Yes, in this case a separate reception card is enclosed with the invitation to the ceremony. The following example shows the most commonly used form:

> *Reception*
> *Immediately following the Ceremony*
> *Knolls Country Club*
> *Lake Forest*
> *The favour of a reply is requested*
> *Lakeside Drive, Lake Forest, Illinois*

Q. *What is the correct form for a single invitation to both the wedding ceremony and the reception?*
A. The card described above may be used when every guest is invited to the reception, but it is more common and less expensive to issue a combined invitation:

> *Mr. and Mrs. Kyle Bennett Farnham*
> *request the honour of your presence*
> *at the marriage of their daughter*
> *Carolyn Ann Jenssen*
> *to*
> *Mr. William Barrett, Junior*
> *Saturday, the fourth of July*
> *at half after three o'clock*
> *Church of the Most Holy Trinity*
> *Montvale, New Jersey*
> *and afterward at the reception*
> *Montvale Country Club*

R.S.V.P.

Q. *We are having a private wedding ceremony with only immediate family present, but would still like to have a reception for family and friends. How would invitations to the reception be worded?*

A. If the invitation is being issued by your parents, it would read:

> *Mr. and Mrs. Scott Turner*
> *request the pleasure of your company*
> *at the wedding reception*
> *of their daughter*
> *Linda Turner Roth*
> *and*
> *Mr. David Huberman*
> *[etc.]*

If you are holding your own reception and the invitations are issued in your name, they would read:

> *The pleasure of your company*
> *is requested*
> *at the wedding reception*
> *of*
> *Linda Turner Roth*
> *and*
> *David Huberman*
> *[etc.]*

Q. *Our ceremony will be followed by a cocktail buffet. Should we say this on the reception invitation?*

A. It is thoughtful to let guests know the extent to which they will be fed during the reception. Use phrases like "cocktail buffet" or "dinner reception" or "luncheon reception" to give your guests a clue as to whether to eat before your reception or plan a meal afterward. This is especially important if the time of your reception would normally indicate that dinner would be served when you are actually planning to serve only light appetizers and wedding cake.

Q. *We are hosting our own wedding. How should the invitation be worded?*

A. Your invitation would read:

> *The honour of your presence*
> *is requested*
> *at the marriage of*
> *Miss Barbara Dillon*
> *to*
> *Mr. Richard McMillan*
> *[etc.]*

[or]

> *Miss Barbara Dillon*
> *and*
> *Mr. Richard McMillan*
> *request the honour of your presence*
> *at their marriage*
> *[etc.]*

If you aren't a "Miss," you may drop the titles (Miss, Mrs., Mr.) from before your names, or you may drop your title but keep the Mr. for the groom's name, if you prefer. If you wish to use a title, it is most usual to use "Mrs. Jennifer Barker Jenson," with your maiden name as your middle name.

Q. *When I was married before, I became estranged from my parents. I am going to be married a second time, and my fiancé's parents are giving our wedding. How should the invitations be worded to indicate that they are doing this?*

A. When the groom's family gives the wedding, the wording may be:

> *Mr. and Mrs. Henry James Sousa*
> *request the honour of your presence*
> *at the marriage of*
> *Pamela Simpson VanReesema*
> *[or Mrs. Pamela Simpson VanReesema]*
> *to*
> *their son*
> *Timothy John Sousa*
> *[etc.]*

Q. *My future husband and I have adult children from earlier marriages. My son is giving our wedding. How should the invitation read:*

A. The invitation may read:

Mr. Louis Carvelas
requests the honour of your presence
at the marriage of his mother
Mrs. Marjorie Wynne
to
Mr. David Hillman
[etc.]

Q. *How should a wedding invitation be worded when . . .*

. . . . the groom's family is co-hosting the wedding?

A.   *Mr. and Mrs. Preston McCloud*
and
Mr. and Mrs. Davidson Gordon
request the pleasure of your company
at the marriage of
Barbara McCloud Wilson
and
Andrew Gordon
[etc.]

. . . . the bride has only one living parent?

A.   *Mrs. [Mr.] Augustus Costa*
requests the honour of your presence
at the marriage of her [his] daughter
Linda Marlene Zimmerman

. . . . the bride has a stepfather?

A. If her own father has had no part in her life, and her stepfather brought her up, the invitation reads:

> *Mr. and Mrs. Bruce Denoyer*
> *request the honour of your presence*
> *at the marriage of their daughter*
> *Francine Ann Colby*
> *[etc.]*

If the bride's mother has been widowed or divorced and has recently remarried, the invitation reads as follows:

> *Mr. and Mrs. Bruce Denoyer*
> *request the honour of your presence*
> *at the marriage of her daughter*
> *[or Mrs. Denoyer's daughter]*
> *Francine Ann Colby*
> *[etc.]*

Q. *My parents are divorced and only my mother is giving my wedding. How should this be indicated on the invitation?*
A. In this case, the invitation would be issued in her name only:

> *Mrs. Ninfa Wagner*
> *requests the honour of your presence*
> *at the marriage of her daughter*
> *[etc.]*

Q. *My parents are divorced and both are remarried. They both, with their spouses, are helping give my*

*wedding, and I would like the invitations to indicate
this. Is there any way to do this?*
A. Yes, all names would be shown on the invitation; with the bride's mother's name listed first:

> *Mr. and Mrs. Deane Flood*
> *and*
> *Mr. and Mrs. William Cook*
> *request the honour of your presence*
> *at the marriage of*
> *Meghan Allison Cook*
> *to*
> *[etc.]*

Q. *My parents divorced several years ago; Dad has
remarried but Mom has not. My father and his new
wife are paying for my wedding, but because we live in
a small town I would like both my parent's names to
appear on the invitation. Dad has graciously agreed to
include Mom's name but said he understood that the
bride's mother's name was always listed first. That
doesn't seem right in this situation. Should my mother's
name be listed before my father's?*
A. When both the bride's parents are sharing expenses equally then, yes, the bride's mother's name
precedes the father's, and she would act as hostess
at the reception. However, when the mother is not
contributing to the expense of the wedding then the
father's name should appear first:

> *Mr. and Mrs. Jonathan Cohen*
> *Mrs. Arlene Cohen*
> *request the honour of your presence*
> *[etc.]*

In this situation, the bride's father and step-mother would host the reception. The bride's mother has no formal role other than as an honored guest.

Q. *I am a widow about to marry again. My parents are giving my wedding, but we don't know how the invitation should be worded so there is no confusion about my name. Are there any guidelines?*

A. Invitations are sent exactly as were the invitations to your first marriage. The only difference is that both your maiden and married names are used:

> *Mr. and Mrs. Hugh Cuthbert*
> *request the honour of your presence*
> *at the marriage of their daughter*
> *Lynn Cuthbert Smythe*
> *[etc.]*

Q. *My fiancé and I are giving our own wedding. May we still send out the invitations in our parents' name?*

A. Yes, you may. It is perfectly proper and a lovely way to include your parents in your happiness.

Q. *Our wedding will be held at a friends' home, although we are paying for it. Are the invitations issued in their name, or in ours?*

A. They are issued in your name. The form would be:

The honour of your presence
is requested
at the marriage of
Coralene Beth Fellows
to
Doctor Frank Highsmith McCullough
Saturday, the second of October
at eight o'clock in the evening
at the residence of Mr. and Mrs. James Dunn
East Lansing, Michigan

R.S.V.P.

Q. My husband and I married in New York three months ago at a civil ceremony and are going to California to visit his parents. They have graciously offered to give a wedding reception for us. How would the invitations be worded?

A. An informal invitation may be issued by using fill-in printed cards and writing "In honor of Mr. and Mrs. Christopher Miller" at the top, or a formal, printed invitation may be used, if the reception is large. It would be worded:

Mr. and Mrs. Dwight Miller
request the pleasure of your company
at a reception
in honor of
Mr. and Mrs. Christopher Miller
[etc.]

Q. *In addition to the guests we would like to invite, are there any others who should receive invitations for any reason?*

A. Yes, the person who performs your ceremony and his or her spouse should receive an invitation. In addition invitations should be sent to:

- The fiancé or live-in companion of an invited guest
- Your bridal party members
- The groom's parents

Q. *My fiancé's aunt is in mourning. Should we send her an invitation?*

A. Yes. It is not up to you to decide for her whether she should attend. She may not wish to, but if you would otherwise invite her, you should do so and let the decision be hers.

Q. *At what age should children receive their own invitations?*

A. Those over the age of ten should, if possible, receive their own invitations. If more than one child in a family is to be invited and you are sending one invitation for all of them, the inner envelope is addressed, "Marion, Richard and Robert" and the outer envelope is addressed, "The Messers. and Miss Dowling" or "Miss Marion Dowling and the Messrs. Robert and Richard Dowling" below.

Q. *We've changed the date of our wedding. Our invitations have already been printed. May we cross out the old date and insert the new one?*

A. You may, but do it neatly. If you have time, you may instead have cards printed to enclose which read, "The date of the wedding has been changed from May tenth to June sixteenth."

Q. *We cancelled our wedding plans shortly after mailing the invitations. How do we inform people?*
A. There are three ways to do this. If you have time, a printed card may be sent:

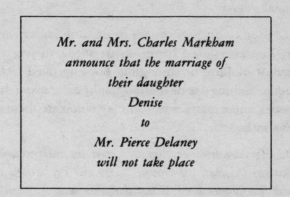

> *Mr. and Mrs. Charles Markham*
> *announce that the marriage of*
> *their daughter*
> *Denise*
> *to*
> *Mr. Pierce Delaney*
> *will not take place*

If time is short, invited guests may be notified by telephone and/or telegram. Telegrams would read, "Regret to inform you wedding of Denise Markham and Pierce Delaney has been canceled," or, to closer friends, "Regret that Denise's and Pierce's wedding has been called off."

Q. *Is it in good taste to enclose reply cards with invitations to a wedding reception?*
A. I have, for years, lamented the use of enclosure

cards, preferring the traditional, third person formal reply to a formal invitation. However, they are widely used and serve a definite purpose—many people today do not bother to answer a wedding invitation promptly by hand, and the use of reply cards ensures that the bride knows in time if invited guests are coming or not. My one caution is not to print the words "number attending ＿＿＿" which could indicate that invited guests may bring additional guests.

Q. *Why are tissues included in wedding invitations?*
A. Engravers used to use tissue sheets to protect against blotting or smudging, but improved techniques and the use of thermography have made the tissues unnecessary and you may eliminate them if you wish.

Q. *My grandmother suggested that we enclose cards that say "within the ribbon" with our invitations to close family members. What does this mean?*
A. This means that a certain number of pews have been reserved for special guests and that they are to sit in one of these pews. The cards are to be taken to the ceremony and shown to the usher who escorts that guest. Another way to be sure special guests are seated close to the front is to alert the head usher who they are so that he is able to watch for them and seat them as you wish.

Q. *What is an at-home card?*
A. It is a card approximately four by two and one

half inches, slightly smaller than the reception card, that notifies your friends of your address after you are married. It is also an ideal way for the bride to let others know if she will be taking her husband's name or continuing to use her current name. It may be included with the invitation or announcement and follows this form:

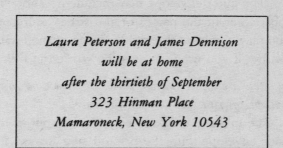

Laura Peterson and James Dennison
will be at home
after the thirtieth of September
323 Hinman Place
Mamaroneck, New York 10543

Q. *Why are there often two envelopes for a wedding invitation?*

A. The practical reason for using two envelopes is that the names of family members, escorts of your invited guests and children can be listed on the inner envelope and just one or two names shown on the addressed, outer envelope which is mailed. The inner envelope is addressed simply, "Mr. and Mrs. O'Donnell," while the outer envelope would be addressed "Mr. and Mrs. David John O'Donnell."

Close relatives' inner envelopes may be addressed "Grandmother," "Aunt Julia and Uncle Edward," etc.

If you are including an invitation to an escort or date on an invitation to a single friend, the outer envelope is addressed to your friend and the inner envelope is addressed, "Miss Richards and guest." If you know his name, use it instead of "guest," and if you know his address, it is preferable to send him his own invitation.

The outer envelope may include no abbreviations either in the names or the street addresses. You may eliminate the middle name of the recipient, but if you use it, it must be written in full.

Q. *How are the invitation, enclosure cards and inner envelope inserted into the mailing envelope?*
A. The invitation, folded edge first, is put in the inner envelope with the printed side toward the flap. The cards are inserted in front of it, with the reception card next to the invitation and any smaller cards in front of that. The inner envelope, unsealed, is placed in the outer envelope with the flap away from you.

Q. *Should wedding invitations have return addresses on the envelope?*
A. Yes. It is required by the United States Postal Service. It is also a way to provide a return address if none appears with the R.S.V.P. on the invitation.

Q. *My fiancé has been married before and we have decided to have a very private ceremony, but we would like to inform friends and family of our marriage. My* *mother suggested that we send announcements. How do announcements differ from invitations?*

A. Announcements are just that—they announce that a wedding has taken place and they are sent after the wedding. It is never mandatory to send them, but they are a useful way to inform friends and acquaintances of your marriage. They are never sent to anyone who has received an invitation to the ceremony and/or the reception.

Q. *Would someone who receives an announcement think we were asking for a wedding gift?*
A. No. Announcements place no obligation on the recipient to send a gift, although he or she may do so.

Q. *How is an announcement worded? Is there different wording for a first and a second wedding?*
A. The form of a wedding announcement resembles the form of the wedding invitation in every way except the wording, which announces rather than invites. It may be issued by the bride and the groom, by the bride's parents, or by both the bride's and groom's parents together. An example is:

Mr. and Mrs. Fernando Costa
and
Mr. and Mrs. Hugo Lamberti
announce the marriage of
Desirée Joan Costa
and
Philip John Lamberti
Saturday, the second of July
One thousand nine hundred and ninety-one
Trinity Church
New Milford, Connecticut

There is no difference in wording for a first or second wedding announcement. Naturally, the bride's name may be different from that of her parents if they issue the announcement, and any wording exceptions used for invitations apply for announcements as well, such as if the bride and groom issue the announcement themselves, if it is issued by their children, or if it is issued by the groom's parents.

An announcement issued by the married couple when the woman has been a widow would read:

Mrs. William Phillip Hoyt
and
Mr. Worthington Adams
announce their marriage
[etc.]

An announcement issued by the married couple when the woman has been previously divorced would read:

Mrs. Mary Brooks
and
Mr. Robert Hanson
announce their marriage
[etc.]

The difference between the two is that a widow would use her former husband's name while a divorcée would use her own first name. The couple may elect not to include titles at all and just use their first names. For example, the first announcement would read, instead:

Claudine Hoyt
and
Worthington Adams
announce their marriage
[etc.]

Q. *How soon after a wedding are announcements sent?*
A. They are preferably mailed the day after the wedding. If there is some extenuating circumstance they may be mailed up to several months later.

Q. *After marrying quietly in a civil ceremony, my husband and I want to send the local newspaper our* *wedding announcement. What should we say in the announcement? Must we mention that it is our second marriage?*

A. Newspapers prefer to receive announcements at least three weeks before the wedding, but will accept it up to one month afterward. Each paper will use as much information as it wishes, and in its own words. Most have forms to be completed by the bride. In general, a younger couple's announcement would include:

- Bride's name and address
- Her parents' names and addresses
- Bride's grandparents names
- Bridegroom's name and address
- His parents' names and their addresses
- Time of ceremony
- Place of ceremony
- Location of reception
- Bride's escort's name
- List of all attendants
- Description of clothing of bride and her attendants
- Bride's schools
- Bride's profession
- Groom's schools
- Groom's profession
- Wedding trip
- Future residence

An older couple's announcement would exclude information on parents, grandparents, and schools and would focus on the ceremony, the professions of the couple, and their future plans.

Most newspapers do not require that you mention whether it is a first or second marriage. It is optional for you to include a statement such as, "Mr. Dwyer's previous marriage ended in divorce." Traditionally such a statement was included to indicate that both parties were legally free to marry.

Q. *We are both widowed after many years of marriage. When we send our announcement to the newspapers may we include the names of our late spouses?*
A. You may, but some papers will not include this information.

Your Ceremony

Q. *I have been married before, with a large wedding. This is my fiancé's first wedding and he would like it to be large, as well. I am concerned that this would not be tasteful and would feel more comfortable having a small, intimate wedding. What should we do?*

A. It used to be that a second wedding was always conducted as a small, private ceremony or a civil ceremony. Recently, however, second weddings with all the fanfare of first weddings have become generally acceptable. Your decision, therefore, depends more on what you are most comfortable doing than it is one of etiquette.

Q. *I have been divorced and plan to marry for the second time. It seems strange to have my father "give me away." Is this necessary?*

A. No, it is not necessary. You certainly may be escorted by your father, or by a son, brother, or close friend, although it is quite acceptable for you to walk alone, or for you to walk with your groom, rather than meeting him at the head of the aisle.

Q. *This is a second wedding for both of us. Should the ceremony include all the elements usually part of a wedding, or may it be abbreviated?*

A. The answer to this question is dependent upon the practices of your priest or rabbi. Generally, your wedding need only include the vows and the sanction of your religion. You may, however, include customs which would be meaningful to you and your groom that are within the guidelines of the religious policy of your faith.

Q. *My fiancé has been married before. He wants to write part of the ceremony to say that he has finally found lasting happiness with me. Is this appropriate?*
A. No. There should be no reference to previous marriages during the wedding ceremony. References invite comparisons which have nothing to do with the fresh start and new life you will be creating together.

Q. *My parents are divorced and each has remarried. Do they sit together during the ceremony?*
A. Absolutely not. They are no longer a couple, and should not be treated as such, even for the wedding of the child they share. Usually, the bride's mother would sit in the front pew with her husband. Members of her immediate family would sit immediately behind them. Your father and his wife would sit in the next pew back, with his family members behind them.

If you have been living with your father and stepmother and have little to do with your own mother, or if your father and stepmother are hosting your wedding, then they would sit in the front pew and your mother and her husband and family would sit further back.

If both your parents are sharing the cost of your wedding, then it is customary for your mother to sit in the front.

Q. *My mother is a widow. I know she is to sit in the front, but is it necessary for her to sit by herself?*
A. No, she should not be expected to sit in lonely

splendor unless it is her choice to do so. A close friend or another family member could certainly be seated with her.

Q. *My fiancé has kept in touch with his late wife's family and they are still close. He would like to invite them to our wedding. Is this appropriate?*

A. Yes. As long as it does not make you uncomfortable, they may certainly be invited. They may not choose to attend, but should not be offended by receiving an invitation. This is especially thoughtful to do if your husband has children from his previous marriage, since it indicates that you and he intend to maintain a relationship with them and not cut them off from their grandchildren.

Q. *My husband and I divorced years ago, but his sister and I were then, and remain, good friends. May I invite her to my wedding?*

A. Yes, you may. If you have maintained a friendship despite your divorce from her brother, then that friendship should not be affected by your new marriage and you are indicating, by inviting her, that you intend to continue it in the future.

Q. *Do friends of the bride always sit on one side of the church and friends of the groom on the other?*

A. They usually do. The left side of the church is the bride's; the right side the groom's. At weddings where the great majority of guests are friends of one family or the other, the ushers may ask some of them if they would mind sitting on the other side.

This not only makes the congregation look more balanced but offers more guests the desirable seats near the aisle.

Q. *Should anyone be seated after the bride's mother is escorted up the aisle?*
A. No, they may not be ushered up the center aisle. If they arrive after the bride's mother is seated, they must stand in the vestibule, go to the balcony, or slip into a rear pew from a side aisle.

Q. *What is the order of attendants in the processional?*
A. The ushers should lead the procession, walking two by two matched by height with the shortest men first. Junior ushers follow the adults. Junior bridesmaids come next. The bridesmaids follow, either singly or in pairs. After the bridesmaids comes the matron of honor, then the maid of honor. A flower girl and finally the ring bearer immediately precede the bride.

Q. *Does the bride walk up the aisle on her escort's right arm or left arm?*
A. She walks on her escort's right arm. When they reach the groom who is standing to the center right at the head of the aisle, she will then be next to him with her right arm free to be given to him. This also allows her escort to reach his seat or her seat in the left pew conveniently.

Q. *I am a widow and plan to be married in a small ceremony with my grown children and close family in attendance. I will not be escorted up the aisle. It seems*

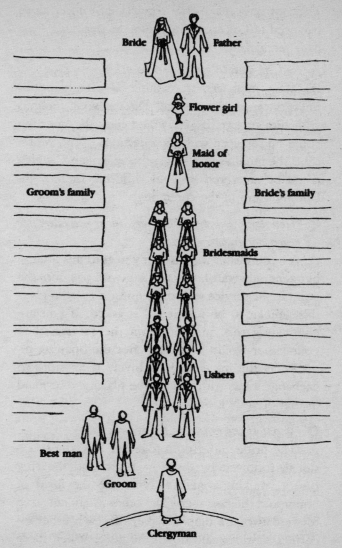

to me that the question, "Who gives this woman . . ." is inappropriate, under the circumstances, and actually ridiculous - I have been living on my own for years. Is it mandatory that it be asked?

A. Most ministers are willing to eliminate this question from the service. Discuss your feelings with him or her. If you would like, the question could be replaced with the question, "Who represents the families in blessing this marriage?" which could be answered by your children, thereby including them in the ceremony.

Q. *How long does my father remain at my side after we reach my groom?*

A. Your minister will instruct you as to this timing, but generally your father remains with you until the point in the service where the question "Who gives this woman to be married?" is asked. If you are eliminating this question from the service, then your father would be seated after the opening remarks by the minister. It is lovely if he stops to exchange a kiss with you before placing your hand in that of your groom.

Q. *What is the order for the recessional?*

A. The bride and groom together lead the recessional, followed by the flower girl and the ring bearer, walking together. Next are the maid of honor and the best man. The other attendants step forward two at a time and pair off, each usher escorting a bridesmaid down the aisle. When there are more ushers than bridesmaids, the extra men follow the couples, walking in pairs. If there is a single man, he walks alone at the end. This is the traditional recessional, although it is acceptable for the wedding party to leave as it entered—bridesmaids together and ushers together—if the bride prefers.

Q. *Is the order of the processional the same for a Jewish wedding as for a Christian ceremony?*
A. No, it differs in that the parents of the bride and the groom are part of the processional for Orthodox and Conservative ceremonies. In most instances, the processional is led by the ushers, fol-

lowed by the bridesmaids. The rabbi comes next, accompanied by the cantor, then the best man, and next the groom, walking between his parents. The maid of honor follows them and the bride, between her parents, comes last.

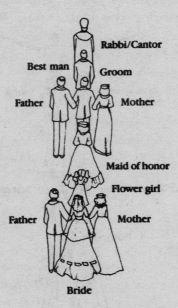

For Reform ceremonies, the groom is ushered by his best man, and the bride by her father. The order of attendants is the same as in a Christian ceremony.

Q. *This is my second marriage, and my fiancé is Catholic. I have received instruction, but have never been to a Catholic wedding. Does it differ from Protestant wedding ceremonies?*

A. The processional, the arrangement of attendants during the ceremony, the recessional and the other details of the ceremony are like those of Protestant weddings. In marriage ceremonies which include participation in a nuptial mass, however, the bridal party is often seated, with the bride and groom seated on two chairs before the altar or kneeling at a kneeling bench. While it is preferred that both the best man and maid of honor be Catholic, at least one should be.

Q. *Is it permissible to have a receiving line at the back of the church, directly following the ceremony?*
A. Yes. This is particularly important if there are many more guests at the ceremony than there will be at the reception, so that they have an opportunity to express their happiness for the bride and groom and so that the newly married couple has the chance to greet them. The receiving line, in order, begins with the bride's mother, followed by the groom's mother, the bride, the groom, and the bride's attendants. Fathers need not stand in the line, although they certainly may. If they do, they stand to the left of their wives.

Q. *Can you help me with a check list for the day of my wedding? I want to be sure nothing is forgotten!*
A. On the day of your wedding:

- Have your hair done or shampoo and arrange it yourself
- Plan to be bathed and dressed at least one hour before the time you will be departing

for the ceremony, or one hour before the photographer arrives if you are having pictures taken at home.

- Pick up any orders that are not to be delivered—flowers, food, etc.
- Have attendants arrive at the place they will dress approximately two hours before the ceremony
- Be sure corsages for women, such as your grandmother, are delivered to the place of the ceremony in the care of the head usher, if they will be arriving there directly
- Remind ushers to arrive at church at least forty-five minutes before the ceremony to plan duties and seat early arrivals
- The groom and best man should be at the place of the ceremony forty-five minutes to one hour before it is to begin
- The best man should check last-minute arrangements with the minister or rabbi and give him or her the fee
- Have cars that will drive you and your wedding party to the ceremony arrive at least one-half hour in advance of the time it will take you to arrive on time for the ceremony

Your Reception

Q. *My first wedding was at home. I am planning to be married again, but my fiancé wants us to have a larger wedding with a reception arranged by a caterer. Are there certain questions we should ask the caterer when discussing plans?*

A. If you and your fiancé have specific ideas about what you would like, explain them to the caterer. If he or she assures you your requests can be met, then review your checklist of twenty key questions before signing a contract:

1. Is there a wedding package? If so, what does it include and what does it cost?
2. Are substitutions permissible?
3. What food and drinks may be selected for the cocktail hour and later in the reception?
4. Will brand-name liquor be served? If not, and you prefer that they are, what is the cost difference? How are cocktails charged—by the drink or by the bottle? If by the bottle, may leftover liquor be returned and credited against the bill?
5. What is the cost of continuing an open bar throughout the reception?
6. If you wish champagne to be poured for a toast, at what point will this be done, and what is the cost?
7. Will the caterer provide a wedding cake if you decide not to provide it yourself from a bakery? Will you be able to sample one of his or her wedding cakes beforehand, if so?

8. How many servers will there be?

9. Will the caterer arrange for floral decorations? If so, does he have a book of arrangements from which to select?

10. If you choose not to have floral decorations for the tables, are candelabra or other centerpieces available?

11. Are there coat check facilities, and if so, is there an extra charge.

12. How will tables be arranged?

13. What is your choice of table linens?

14. Is there an option to extend the reception an extra hour? At what cost?

15. At what time do servers go on overtime pay?

16. Are gratuities included in the total package?

17. Are there adequate parking facilities and if so, is there a charge or is valet parking available?

18. Will the caterer provide printed directions to the catering hall for you to include with your invitations?

19. What is the charge for providing food and beverages for the photographer and musicians?

20. What is the deadline for your guest count?

It is also important to ask the last date you may cancel, and what, if any, the charge would be were you to do so. Be absolutely sure that every service to be provided and the total itemized costs are given to you in a contract and that you read it carefully before you sign it.

Q. *Although gratuities for the servers and bartenders are included in the caterer's fee, do I also tip the caterer?*
A. It is not necessary to tip the caterer since he or she is presumably the owner of the business.

Q. *Our reception will be held at my fiancé's club. The manager has been wonderful in helping with all the arrangements. Do we tip him? If so, how much?*
A. A tip is in order, with the size depending on the amount of extra effort he has made on your behalf. If your guests number more than a few, his gratuity would be anywhere from $50 to $100.

Q. *Our reception will be held in the church social hall, with friends and family providing the refreshments. How should I thank them for doing this?*
A. Thank them in person during the reception, trying to mention what they brought. As soon as possible afterward, send a thank you note to them for helping to make your wedding celebration so memorable for you.

Q. *My future husband and I have both been married before, both at very large and formal weddings. This time we are having a civil service, followed by dinner at a restaurant for our families and a few friends. We are on a limited budget and don't know how to handle ordering, etc. Do you have any suggestions?*
A. You and your groom should find out ahead of time what facilities are offered, to see if it is possible to reserve a small, private room and then order

what you wish to be served. Most restaurants will allow a choice in the same price range, and this avoids any question of how costly a meal the guests might order and eliminates any complications in paying the check. You may order wine or champagne for the group. You may also pay for cocktails, or guests may order and pay for them themselves if they are not offered. You should have a wedding cake, no matter how small, which the restaurant may provide, or which you may provide from a bakery, after discussing this possibility with the restaurant management.

Q. *My fiancé and I plan to be married at a small ceremony in the town where we live. I have been married before and don't feel comfortable inviting all the same people who attended my first wedding to this one. He has not, however, and his parents, who live quite a distance away, would like to have a reception for us several weeks after our ceremony, in their town. They want me to wear my wedding gown and have invited my attendants, as well. Is this appropriate?*

A. Yes, it is lovely that your groom's parents would like you to appear as your husband's bride, and it is perfectly appropriate for you to wear your wedding gown. You should not, however, attempt to include your bridesmaids, who would have to travel and incur more expense, or to re-enact your wedding. Your new parents-in-law may have a "wedding cake," if they wish, but otherwise the party should be much like any other held to celebrate a special event.

Q. *Because my fiancé and I have been married before, we are having a small, private ceremony, after which we plan a two-week trip. We would like to have a party for friends and family when we return, but don't want anyone to bring gifts, and don't plan to set it up as a belated reception with a wedding cake or wedding-related activities. May we do this? If so, how do we word the invitations?*

A. Yes, you may do this. You simply send invitations for a party without mentioning that it is a celebration of your marriage. If you will be away when people might be responding, direct R.s.v.p.'s to a friend or family member, who can respond to guest's questions as to whether they should bring a gift, etc. by explaining that you want to share your happiness and don't wish guest's presents—just their presence.

Q. *We are planning an informal reception after our wedding ceremony. Is it necessary to have a receiving line?*

A. No, it is not. You and your groom may simply greet guests together at the door and let your wedding party and parents mingle, or you may dispense with welcoming guests in this fashion entirely. If you do, you must be sure to speak to each guest before the reception is over.

Q. *If we have a receiving line, what is the order in which we stand?*

A. The bride's mother is first in line, followed by the groom's mother. The presence of fathers in the receiving line is optional, but if one father is present, the other should be as well. The bride's father would stand after the bride's mother, followed by the groom's mother, the groom's father, the bride, then the groom. Next is the bride's honor attendant, and then the bridesmaids, whose presence is optional. A waiter is positioned near the end of the receiving line to offer champagne, punch or other beverages to those who have passed through.

Q. *My parents are divorced and my father has remarried. Should both his wife and my mother be in the receiving line? Should my father?*

A. No. Divorced parents do not stand in the receiving line together. If the bride's mother and stepfather are giving the wedding, she alone or both are in the line—but not the bride's father. If her father and stepmother are giving the wedding, they, as host and hostess, stand in line, and the bride's mother is simply an honored guest. If neither has remarried, only the bride's mother should be in the line unless the father is giving the reception. In that case, the estranged wife would not act as hostess, but the godmother of the bride, or an aunt, or even a very close family friend would receive in her place. When the groom's parents are divorced, his mother joins him in the line, and neither his father nor his stepfather need be there, which eliminates any complications.

Q. *Is it necessary to have a guest book at the reception?*
A. No, it is not necessary, but it is a nice custom and gives you a written record of your guests. Supervision of the guest book table is a pleasant task to assign your or your groom's children, or a bridesmaid may attend to it instead. It should be placed on a table near the receiving line and, as the guests arrive and join the line, the child or attendant supervising the book reminds each one (or one member of each couple) to sign.

Q. *We are planning a rather large reception and a formal dinner, so we would like to have a table for the bridal party. Is there a particular seating order for this table?*
A. Yes, there is a traditional seating plan. The bride and groom sit at the center, facing out so that the guests can see them. No one is seated opposite them. The bride sits on the groom's right, with the best man on her right; the maid of honor sits on the groom's left; and the bridesmaids and ushers alternate along the same side of the table. Husbands, wives, and fiancé's of the attendants also sit at the bride's table. If there are too many people to fit along one side, the table should form a "U," so that guests may sit at the two arms rather than obstruct anyone's view of the bride and the groom. When possible, children of the bride and groom from previous marriages should be seated at this table, too.

Two ways to form the receiving line

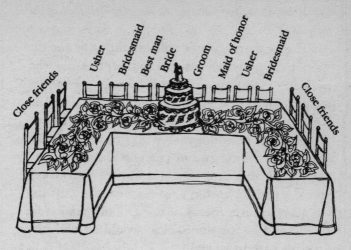

The bride's table

Q. *My mother has remarried and I don't get along at all with her husband. I do not want him at my reception but my mother is insisting that she won't come without him. What can I do?*

A. Your situation requires that you have another conversation with your mother in as unemotional a way as possible. Tell her that you love her very much and can't imagine being married without her there, but that you simply cannot have her husband with her because it would upset you too much. Tell her you will tell her husband the same thing so that she is not put in the position of having to do so. If she still refuses, it becomes her choice and you may have to face the possibility that she will not attend.

Q. *Who sits at the parents' table or tables during the reception?*

A. The mother and father of both the bride and the groom, the grandparents, the minister or rabbi who performs the ceremony and his or her spouse are included. If there is room, godparents, relatives and close family friends are also seated at this table.

At large receptions there may be separate parents' tables for the groom's parents and the bride's parents. In this case, grandparents of the groom would sit at the groom's parents' table, etc. If the clergyperson is a friend of the groom's family, he or she and his or her spouse would sit with the groom's parents as well.

Q. *Both of my parents and both of my fiancé's parents were divorced, and all have remarried. It is a nightmare trying to plan seating at the reception for them. What should we do?*

A. What you should not do is expect your parents and their ex-spouses to sit together. If your reception is large enough, each couple should be at its own table, seated with appropriate family members. If your reception is small and there will not be enough tables for them to be separated, then put one of your sets of parents with one of your fiancé's sets of parents. For example, seat your mother and her husband with his mother and her husband and your father and his wife with your groom's father and his wife.

Q. *Are toasts in order at the reception?*

A. Yes, they are. This is a celebration that calls for

toasts, which are traditionally made with champagne, but which may be made with punch or a sparkling juice drink instead. The best man is the first to toast the couple, and his toast may be followed by others, including you to your groom or he to you.

Q. *What sort of toasts are appropriate for a second wedding?*
A. Exactly the same kind of toasts that are appropriate for a first wedding. A best man's toast to the bridal couple may be something like: "To Jessica and Michael—may they always share the love and happiness we are all sharing today." It should never refer to previous marriages or mention "the second time around," which would be inappropriate and in poor taste. The prime ingredient in an appropriate toast is that the sentiment be from the heart.

Q. *Are congratulatory telegrams read aloud?*
A. Yes, they are read by the best man following the toasts. He then gives the telegrams to the bride's parents for safekeeping until the bride and groom return from their honeymoon and are able to acknowledge them or, if the bride has no parents, directly to the groom.

Q. *What is the procedure for cutting the wedding cake?*
A. The first cut is made by the bride and groom, his right hand over hers. It should be cut early in the reception if only hors d'oeuvres are being served, or after the meal as the dessert course for

longer receptions. Since most guests feel they cannot leave until the cake is cut, however, don't wait too late to cut it.

Traditionally, the groom cuts a small piece of cake from the first slice and feeds it to the bride, and then the bride feeds him a small piece. This tradition, if included, should never, ever include the squishing of cake and icing into one another's faces.

Q. *What is a groom's cake?*

A. One traditional form is a fruit cake. Slices are cut and put into individual white boxes, tied with white satin ribbon and decorated with the combined initials of the bride and groom. These boxes are placed on a table near the door, and each departing guest is expected to take one as a memento of the wedding. This has become a very expensive tradition, however, and is often replaced, if a groom's cake is offered at all, by a chocolate cake, placed on a separate table from the wedding cake. It is not cut by the couple or served, as is the wedding cake, but it is sliced by a waiter so that guests who prefer it are free to help themselves.

Q. *My fiancé and I plan to have dancing at our reception, but don't know how to handle the traditional sequence of partners. I have both a stepfather and natural father, he has a stepmother and a natural mother. Who should dance with whom first?*

A. I would really advise that you forgo this process entirely and instead simply have a first dance with your groom, during or after which you have instructed your attendants to join you to indicate that everyone is to begin dancing. It is much too complicated for you to try to dance with both fathers or for your groom to try to dance with both his mothers, or to choose with whom you each dance first.

Q. *I would like a photograph of my groom and me with my parents, although they are divorced. Is this all right?*

A. No, it is not. Many people will argue that they are still your parents and that you have the right to have this picture taken, but you have to realize that they are no longer a couple and you shouldn't request that they appear as one. Instead, have separate pictures taken, one with you and your groom and your mother, and then one of the two of you with your father.

Q. *Should my stepfather appear in a photograph with my groom, me, and my mother?*

A. Certainly, assuming he is on friendly terms with you. It would be meaningful to your mother to have this picture, and there is no reason not to support her and her marriage in this way.

Q. *My husband's former wife is deceased. He is close to his former in-laws. We invited them to our wedding because he has remained close to them and they are the grandparents of his children, but I don't know what to say to them. Is there anything special I should say?*

A. You should be charming and gracious and tell them how glad you are that they are sharing this day with you. If you can, you could also tell them you are looking forward to getting to know them better when they come to visit you and the children. You absolutely should not be apologetic or offer comparisons between this wedding and your husband's previous wedding, even if you feel it is foremost on their minds.

Q. *My future husband's ex-wife is threatening to come to our wedding and reception. I am so worried that she will create an unpleasant scene. What should we do?*
A. The only thing you can do is notify the club manager or caterer that you are hiring a security guard specifically to keep her out, and then do so. You can get a legal restraining order against her. While that won't necessarily keep her away it will enable the manager or caterer to call the police if she appears.

Q. *We are not having a large wedding or attendants other than a matron of honor and a best man, but we are having a fairly sizable reception and my fiancé's children will be there. Where should we have them seated during the reception?*
A. If possible, have a separate bridal party table and seat them with you and your groom and the best man, his wife or date, and the matron of honor and her husband. Otherwise, seat them with grandparents or close relatives with whom they are comfortable, and be sure to visit with them frequently throughout the reception. Be sure you have pictures taken of all of you together when arranging group portraits.

Q. *My children are giving a reception for my new husband and me. We weren't planning on having a reception at all, and I am not sure what will be expected of us. For example, should we cut the wedding cake together, and is it necessary for me to throw my bouquet at the end?*

A. Yes, you should cut the cake together, but no, you needn't throw your bouquet. You may, of course, do so and it is likely that everyone would love to see you carry out that tradition, but if it makes you uncomfortable it is completely unnecessary.

Q. *When does the bride throw the bouquet?*

A. After the cake is cut and before the bride leaves to change her clothes.

Q. *Both my future husband and I have been married before and still live in the same town we always have. Our former spouses are deceased. Our children are insisting on planning a small wedding and reception for us, which we appreciate, but we absolutely do not want anyone to bring us gifts. We don't need a thing, and all our friends have known us for years. Many of them were a part of our previous weddings, in fact. May we ask our children to write "no gifts, please" on the invitations?*

A. Yes, you may. It is unusual, but many people will honor the request. Some will want to give you a gift despite the request. If they do, be sure to accept it graciously—gift giving and weddings are hard to separate.

Q. *Should we give favors to our wedding guests?*
A. This is frequently a practice among many ethnic groups and whether or not you choose to give them will depend upon tradition within your family. Favors vary from a small, wrapped piece of cake to a small box of chocolates wrapped in ribbon to ceramic figures to a bottle of champagne. If given, they are given when the guests line up to say good-bye to the bride and groom (and often give them gifts of money) or they are given by a waiter or a member of the family at the door as guests depart.

Wedding Gifts

Q. *Are gifts required for a second wedding?*

A. No, but close friends and relatives may want to give you something special to commemorate your marriage, and others may feel awkward not giving a gift, so will send one anyway.

Q. *My fiancé and I can't think of a thing we need since we both have complete households already and actually have to get rid of things that are duplicates, but friends are insisting they want to give us wedding gifts. Do you have any suggestions as to what we should tell them?*

A. You may use the gift registry services at local stores to help them in their selection, or, if either of you have children from previous marriage, you could suggest gifts which include them. These gifts, while not traditional tableware or appliances, could be games, electronic games, tickets to a local event, gift certificates for a favorite restaurant, camping equipment, or hobby items such as camera accessories (for taking pictures of your new family), etc. Other gifts might be promises of babysitting, or missing pieces from your existing china, crystal or silver patterns. Additionally, picnic baskets, wine and spirits, or baskets of gourmet foods are gifts you surely will be able to use.

Q. *I've received an invitation to a wedding but not to the reception. Must I send a gift?*

A. No. There is no obligation attached to an invitation to the wedding only, although you may send a gift if you wish.

Q. *My fiancé and I will be married at a small cere-mony with only family members in attendance. We would like to share our news with friends by sending announcements, but want to be sure they don't feel they have to send us a gift, particularly since many of them sent me presents the first time I was married. Does receiving an announcement obligate them to send a gift?*

A. No. As with an invitation to the wedding only, the receipt of an announcement does not demand a gift in return.

Q. *How much should be spent on a wedding gift?*

A. There is no "formula" to determine the amount you should spend on a wedding gift. Many people today try to figure out what is being spent on them as a guest at the reception and match that amount. This is not appropriate, and the size or elaborate-ness of the wedding should have nothing to do with the amount spent or given. The decision should be based on a combination of two things - affection for the bride, groom, or their families, and one's fi-nancial capacity.

When attending a second wedding for a bride or groom whose first wedding you also attended, a gift is not required, but may certainly be given. In this case, a token of your affection, which could be a framed photograph of the new bride and groom or a special memento of some aspect of their rela-tionship together is thoughtful.

Q. *How do I know when to give money as a wedding present and when to give a gift?*

A. This is determined by tradition, ethnic custom, or the circumstances of the bride and groom. A gift of money may be earmarked for a specific purpose—such as toward the purchase of new furniture—or it may be given with no designation for its use.

Q. *Should a check given as a wedding gift be mailed or taken to the wedding?*
A. If it is a customary in your area to give money as a gift, it is usually taken to the reception. As the reception draws to a close, a line of guests forms near the bridal table and an envelope containing a card and the check given to the bride or groom. Checks may be sent to the couple before the wedding, however, in which case the donor would still go through the line to bid farewell to the bride and groom and to wish them well.

Q. *Friends have asked how checks given as wedding presents should be made out. What should we tell them?*
A. When given before the wedding they are made out to either the bride, or to both the bride and groom in their own names. When they are given at the reception, they are made out to the bride and groom in their married names, assuming the bride is changing her name, or if she is not, in her unchanged name and his name.

Q. *When a couple to be married has been living together and the invitations are sent by them, where* *should gifts be sent—to them, or to the bride's mother's home?*

A. They should be sent to the couple, addressed to the bride. When they are sent after the wedding takes place, they are addressed to both.

Q. *Our nephew is marrying a woman who has been married before and whom we have never met. May we send our wedding gift, which is really for him, directly to him, or must it be sent to her, and if so, in what name?*

A. The gift should be sent to the bride, even though it is intended for your nephew. It should be addressed to the name she is using now, whether she has reverted to her maiden name or is still using her married name from her previous marriage. The name she is using would be written on the wedding invitation you received.

Q. *My future husband and I have received several wedding gifts which duplicate things we already have from our previous marriages. May they be exchanged?*

A. Yes, they may be exchanged. Whether or not you inform the donor of your action is entirely up to you, but a thank you note should be written in any event.

Q. *When a wedding gift arrives broken, what should we do?*

A. If the gift has been mailed by the store, take it back to the store and have it replaced, without mentioning the fact to the donor. If the package was

mailed by the donor and it was insured, the donor
should be notified so that he or she can collect the
insurance. If it was not insured, say nothing, since
the donor would then feel obligated to replace the
gift at a duplicate expense.

Q. *When should thank-you notes be sent?*
A. As soon as possible. You should write your
notes on the day the gift arrives if possible, both as
a courtesy to the sender who will be anxious to
know it arrived, and to keep yourself from becoming inundated with notes to write after the honeymoon. In ordinary circumstances, all thank-you
notes should be sent within three months of the
date of the wedding.

Q. *Are thank-you notes signed by both the bride and
the groom?*
A. It is preferable for one to sign with a reference
in the text to the other, such as, "Hans and I both
thank you for . . ." or "With love from both of us,
Samantha."

Q. *May the groom write any of the thank-you notes?*
A. Indeed, yes. There is no reason the groom
should not share this task, especially when the notes
are for his relatives and friends who really don't
know the bride.

Q. *Are printed thank-you cards an acceptable way of
acknowledging wedding presents?*
A. No. Every present must be acknowledged by a
personal, handwritten note. If printed cards are

used, a personal note, mentioning the gift specifically, must be added.

Q. *Should wedding presents be opened at the reception?*
A. No. It is better to wait until later so that the bride and groom may use their time at the reception to talk with their guests. Any gifts brought to the reception should be gathered up by one of the attendants, assisting the bride and groom or their parents, and kept for the bride and groom to open later.

Index

Index